THE ULTIMATE
SECOND GRADE
MATH WORKBOOK

ISBN: 9781947569492
27 26 25 24 23 10 11 12 13 14

Printed in China

Time to warm up! Fill in the blanks to add.

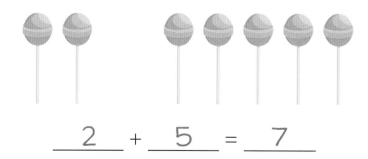

$$\underline{2} + \underline{5} = \underline{7}$$

$$\underline{} + \underline{} = \underline{}$$

$$\underline{} + \underline{} = \underline{}$$

$$\underline{} + \underline{} = \underline{}$$

Fill in the blanks to add.

_____ + _____ = _____

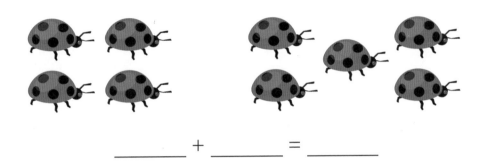

_____ + _____ = _____

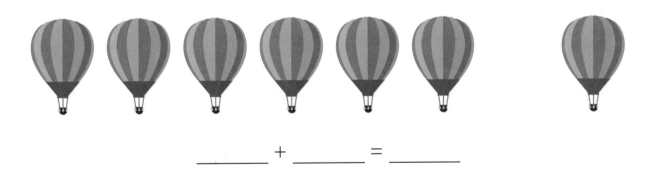

_____ + _____ = _____

For more practice, visit IXL.com or the IXL mobile app and enter this code in the search bar.

IXL.com skill ID

T2B

You can use a number line to show addition. Try it for 2 + 5. First, start at 2. Now, count on by 5. Look at the number you land on.

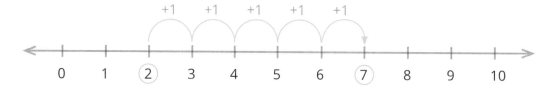

You land on the number 7! So, 2 + 5 = 7.

Fill in the blanks to add.

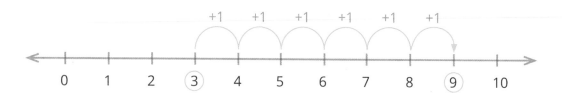

3 + 6 = 9

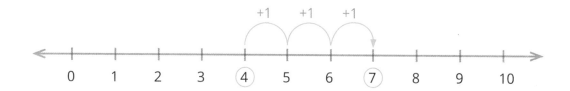

_____ + _____ = _____

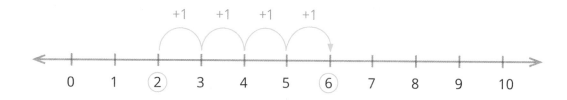

_____ + _____ = _____

Number lines

Fill in the blanks to add.

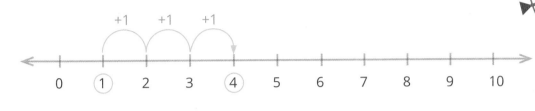

_____ + _____ = _____

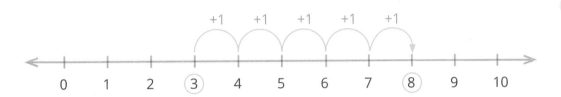

_____ + _____ = _____

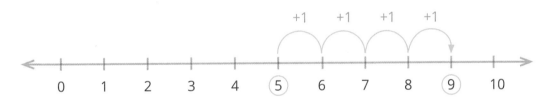

_____ + _____ = _____

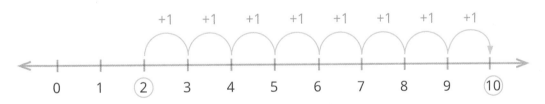

_____ + _____ = _____

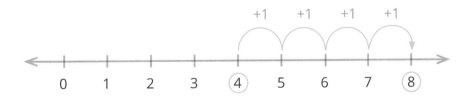

_____ + _____ = _____

IXL.com
skill ID
UWW

Add.

6 + 2 = __8__

3 + 1 = _____

4 + 4 = _____

5 + 2 = _____

4 + 2 = _____

3 + 2 = _____

1 + 7 = _____

4 + 6 = _____

6 + 3 = _____

3 + 4 = _____

2 + 7 = _____

6 + 1 = _____

4 + 0 = _____

5 + 4 = _____

Add.

7 + 2 = _____

9 + 1 = _____

2 + 3 = _____

0 + 8 = _____

1 + 8 = _____

3 + 5 = _____

8 + 2 = _____

9 + 0 = _____

7 + 1 = _____

2 + 2 = _____

5 + 5 = _____

1 + 5 = _____

IXL.com
skill ID
WUL

Let's Learn!

You can add numbers in any order! The sum will be the same.

$$3 + 5 = 8 \qquad\qquad 5 + 3 = 8$$

Add.

2 + 5 = ___7___

5 + 2 = ___7___

7 + 2 = _____

2 + 7 = _____

9 + 1 = _____

1 + 9 = _____

4 + 2 = _____

2 + 4 = _____

8 + 0 = _____

0 + 8 = _____

3 + 6 = _____

6 + 3 = _____

7 + 3 = _____

3 + 7 = _____

IXL.com
skill ID
YDX

Fill in the blank for the first addition sentence. Then rewrite to add in a different order.

3 + __4__ = 7

__4__ + __3__ = 7

4 + _____ = 5

_____ + _____ = 5

5 + _____ = 9

_____ + _____ = 9

8 + _____ = 10

_____ + _____ = 10

6 + _____ = 8

_____ + _____ = 8

9 + _____ = 9

_____ + _____ = 9

2 + _____ = 5

_____ + _____ = 5

1 + _____ = 8

_____ + _____ = 8

Complete the doubles facts.

2 + 2 = ____4____

5 + 5 = _____

3 + 3 = _____

1 + 1 = _____

6 + 6 = _____

4 + 4 = _____

8 + 8 = _____

9 + 9 = _____

7 + 7 = _____

10 + 10 = _____

Complete the doubles facts.

_____3_____ + _____3_____ = 6   _____ + _____ = 2

_____ + _____ = 8   _____ + _____ = 12

_____ + _____ = 18   _____ + _____ = 4

_____ + _____ = 10   _____ + _____ = 16

_____ + _____ = 14   _____ + _____ = 20

Let's Learn!

You can use doubles facts to help add numbers that are close to doubles. Try it for 3 + 4.

You know 3 + 3 = 6. So, 3 + 4 is equal to 3 + 3, plus one more.

That means 3 + 4 = 7!

Complete the doubles and near doubles facts.

6 + 6 = __12__   4 + 4 = _____   7 + 7 = _____

6 + 7 = __13__   4 + 5 = _____   7 + 8 = _____

5 + 5 = _____   9 + 9 = _____   8 + 8 = _____

5 + 6 = _____   9 + 10 = _____   8 + 9 = _____

IXL.com
skill ID
XAY

Complete the doubles and near doubles facts.

5 + 5 = _____   9 + 10 = _____

6 + 7 = _____   4 + 4 = _____

8 + 8 = _____   5 + 6 = _____

7 + 8 = _____   7 + 7 = _____

6 + 6 = _____   9 + 9 = _____

8 + 9 = _____   4 + 5 = _____

Addition with 10 can make other problems easier. Practice making a 10.

7 + _____ = 10   2 + _____ = 10

6 + _____ = 10   9 + _____ = 10

5 + _____ = 10   8 + _____ = 10

3 + _____ = 10   4 + _____ = 10

Practice adding from 10.

10 + 2 = _____   10 + 3 = _____   10 + 6 = _____

10 + 9 = _____   10 + 5 = _____   10 + 10 = _____

10 + 8 = _____   10 + 1 = _____   10 + 7 = _____

When you add beyond 10, you can make a 10 to help. Try it with 7 + 5.

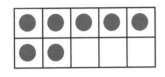 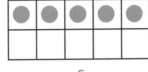

7 + 5

Show 7 + 5 with counters.

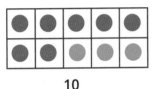 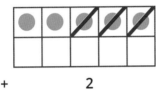

10 + 2

Since 7 + 3 = 10, move 3 counters over to make a 10. There are 2 counters left over.

So, 7 + 5 = 10 + 2 = 12.

Add by making a 10.

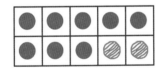 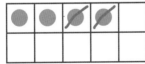

$8 + 4 = 10 + \underline{\quad 2 \quad} = \underline{\quad 12 \quad}$

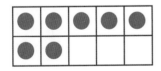 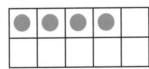

$7 + 4 = 10 + \underline{\qquad} = \underline{\qquad}$

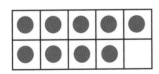 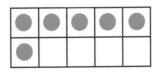

$9 + 6 = 10 + \underline{\qquad} = \underline{\qquad}$

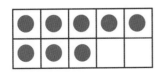 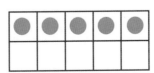

$8 + 5 = 10 + \underline{\qquad} = \underline{\qquad}$

Add by making a 10.

8 + 6 = 10 + __4__ = __14__   9 + 2 = 10 + _____ = _____

9 + 4 = 10 + _____ = _____   8 + 7 = 10 + _____ = _____

6 + 5 = 10 + _____ = _____   7 + 6 = 10 + _____ = _____

9 + 3 = 10 + _____ = _____   9 + 8 = 10 + _____ = _____

9 + 9 = 10 + _____ = _____   8 + 3 = 10 + _____ = _____

7 + 5 = 10 + _____ = _____   9 + 7 = 10 + _____ = _____

5 + 9 = 10 + _____ = _____   8 + 4 = 10 + _____ = _____

Add. Make a 10 to help!

9 + 6 = _____

8 + 6 = _____

7 + 4 = _____

5 + 7 = _____

8 + 9 = _____

6 + 9 = _____

9 + 5 = _____

6 + 7 = _____

6 + 8 = _____

8 + 5 = _____

7 + 8 = _____

5 + 6 = _____

5 + 8 = _____

7 + 9 = _____

Add.

3 + 6 = _____   4 + 8 = _____

7 + 7 = _____   3 + 7 = _____

9 + 8 = _____   8 + 6 = _____

5 + 4 = _____   9 + 3 = _____

8 + 7 = _____   3 + 5 = _____

6 + 7 = _____   8 + 2 = _____

8 + 8 = _____   9 + 9 = _____

4 + 7 = _____   9 + 7 = _____

IXL.com
skill ID
MQX

Answer each question.

There are 7 people on a bus. Then 5 more people get on. How many people are on the bus now?

_____ people

Jamie and Alex have an apple tree in their yard. Jamie picks 8 apples from the tree. Alex picks 6 apples. How many apples do they pick in all?

_____ apples

Tia sold 9 cups of lemonade in the morning. She sold 5 more cups in the afternoon. How many cups of lemonade did Tia sell in all?

_____ cups

Zoe is baking pies for a pie-eating contest. She baked 6 pies on Saturday and 7 pies on Sunday. How many pies did Zoe bake in all?

_____ pies

Mr. White is gathering wooden boards to make a tree house. He found 9 boards in the shed. He found 8 more boards in the garage. How many boards does Mr. White have?

IXL.com
skill ID
EN6

_____ boards

Fill in the blanks to subtract.

$$\underline{\ 6\ } - \underline{\ 2\ } = \underline{\ 4\ }$$

$$\underline{\hspace{2cm}} - \underline{\hspace{1.5cm}} = \underline{\hspace{1.5cm}}$$

$$\underline{\hspace{2cm}} - \underline{\hspace{1.5cm}} = \underline{\hspace{1.5cm}}$$

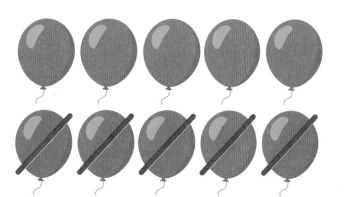

$$\underline{\hspace{2cm}} - \underline{\hspace{1.5cm}} = \underline{\hspace{1.5cm}}$$

Fill in the blanks to subtract.

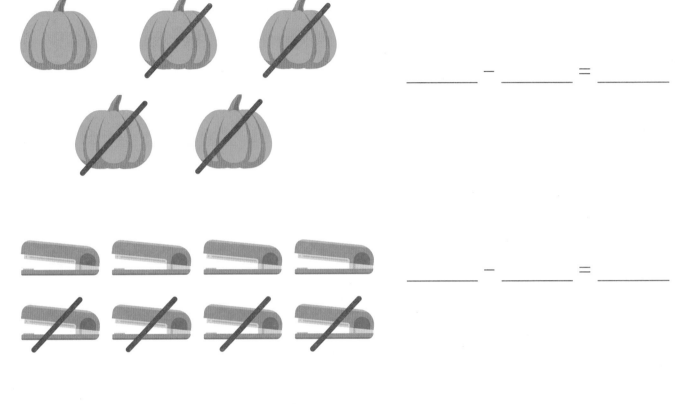

_____ − _____ = _____

_____ − _____ = _____

_____ − _____ = _____

For more practice, visit IXL.com or the IXL mobile app and enter this code in the search bar.

IXL.com
skill ID
VY2

Let's Learn!

You can use a number line to show subtraction. Try it with 9 – 5. First, start at 9. Then, count back by 5. Look at the number you land on.

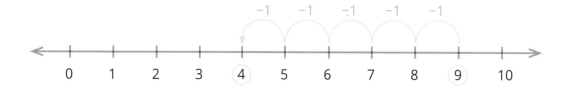

You land on the number 4! So, 9 – 5 = 4.

Fill in the blanks to subtract.

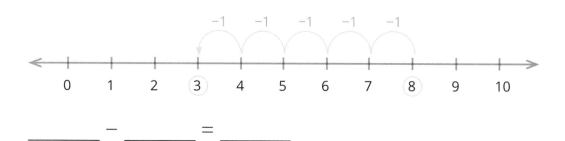

__7__ – __6__ = __1__

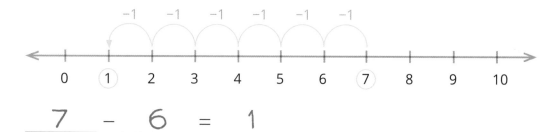

_____ – _____ = _____

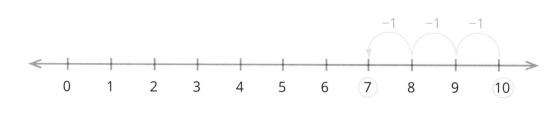

_____ – _____ = _____

Fill in the blanks to subtract.

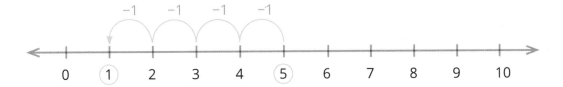

_____ − _____ = _____

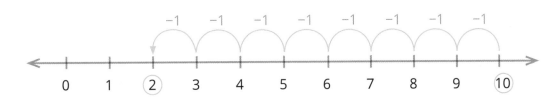

_____ − _____ = _____

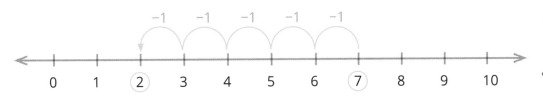

_____ − _____ = _____

_____ − _____ = _____

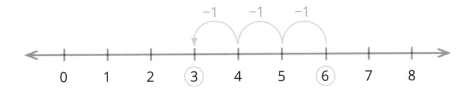

_____ − _____ = _____

Subtract.

9 − 3 = __6__   5 − 2 = _____

8 − 1 = _____   7 − 5 = _____

6 − 5 = _____   4 − 1 = _____

9 − 4 = _____   8 − 2 = _____

10 − 4 = _____   5 − 3 = _____

7 − 2 = _____   10 − 8 = _____

4 − 0 = _____   8 − 6 = _____

Subtract.

6 − 4 = _____

8 − 5 = _____

3 − 3 = _____

7 − 1 = _____

10 − 6 = _____

10 − 2 = _____

8 − 7 = _____

9 − 6 = _____

6 − 3 = _____

5 − 5 = _____

9 − 7 = _____

9 − 2 = _____

6 − 0 = _____

5 − 1 = _____

9 − 8 = _____

10 − 5 = _____

Let's Learn!

Addition and subtraction are related. Subtraction can undo addition! For example, start with 3. You can *add* 4 to get 7.

 $3 + 4 = 7$

To get back to 3, just *subtract* 4.

 $7 - 4 = 3$

Solve the related addition and subtraction facts.

$9 + 1 = \underline{10}$ $6 + 3 = \underline{}$ $4 + 4 = \underline{}$

$10 - 1 = \underline{9}$ $9 - 3 = \underline{}$ $8 - 4 = \underline{}$

$5 + 6 = \underline{}$ $7 + 5 = \underline{}$ $8 + 7 = \underline{}$

$11 - 5 = \underline{}$ $12 - 5 = \underline{}$ $15 - 8 = \underline{}$

Write a related addition or subtraction fact.

3 + 5 = 8

___8___ – ___5___ = ___3___

7 – 1 = 6

___6___ + ___1___ = ___7___

3 + 6 = 9

_____ – _____ = _____

9 + 4 = 13

_____ – _____ = _____

13 – 5 = 8

_____ + _____ = _____

5 + 6 = 11

_____ – _____ = _____

16 – 9 = 7

_____ + _____ = _____

15 – 6 = 9

_____ + _____ = _____

18 – 9 = 9

_____ + _____ = _____

8 + 7 = 15

_____ – _____ = _____

IXL.com
skill ID
DM2

Let's Learn!

A **fact family** is a group of math facts that use the same numbers.

Let's find the fact family for 3, 6, and 9. The fact family has two addition facts.

$$3 + 6 = 9 \qquad 6 + 3 = 9$$

The fact family has two subtraction facts.

$$9 - 3 = 6 \qquad 9 - 6 = 3$$

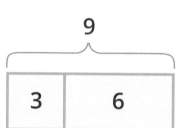

Complete each fact family.

2, 9, 11
_2_ + _9_ = _11_
_9_ + _2_ = _11_
_11_ – _2_ = _9_
_11_ – _9_ = _2_

7, 3, 4
_____ + _____ = _____
_____ + _____ = _____
_____ – _____ = _____
_____ – _____ = _____

IXL.com
skill ID
NSN

Complete each fact family.

12, 4, 8

_____ + _____ = _____

_____ + _____ = _____

_____ − _____ = _____

_____ − _____ = _____

5, 7, 12

_____ + _____ = _____

_____ + _____ = _____

_____ − _____ = _____

_____ − _____ = _____

7, 8, 15

_____ + _____ = _____

_____ + _____ = _____

_____ − _____ = _____

_____ − _____ = _____

17, 9, 8

_____ + _____ = _____

_____ + _____ = _____

_____ − _____ = _____

_____ − _____ = _____

9, 19, 10

_____ + _____ = _____

_____ + _____ = _____

_____ − _____ = _____

_____ − _____ = _____

6, 8, 14

_____ + _____ = _____

_____ + _____ = _____

_____ − _____ = _____

_____ − _____ = _____

Subtraction with 10 can make other problems easier. Subtract from 10.

$10 - 4 =$ _____ $10 - 2 =$ _____

$10 - 1 =$ _____ $10 - 7 =$ _____

$10 - 5 =$ _____ $10 - 8 =$ _____

Fill in the missing number to make 10.

$17 -$ _____ $= 10$ $11 -$ _____ $= 10$

$18 -$ _____ $= 10$ _____ $- 9 = 10$

_____ $- 6 = 10$ $13 -$ _____ $= 10$

$10 -$ _____ $= 10$ _____ $- 4 = 10$

Let's Learn!

You can use counters to make a 10 to help subtract. Try it with 13 − 7.

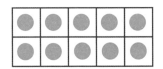 

Start with 13 counters. To make a 10, cross off 3 counters.

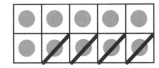 

You already crossed off 3. To subtract 7 in all, cross off 4 more.

This shows that 13 − 7 is the same as 10 − 4. So, 13 − 7 = 6.

Subtract by making a 10.

15 − 8 = ?

15 − ___5___ − ___3___ = ?

10 − ___3___ = ___7___

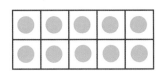 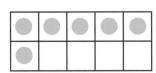

16 − 8 = ?

16 − _____ − _____ = ?

10 − _____ = _____

 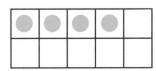

14 − 9 = ?

14 − _____ − _____ = ?

10 − _____ = _____

Subtract by making a 10.

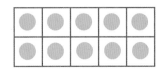 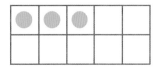

13 − 6 = ?

13 − _____ − _____ = ?

10 − _____ = _____

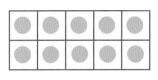

15 − 6 = ?

15 − _____ − _____ = ?

10 − _____ = _____

Subtract by making a 10.

13 − 4 = ?

__13__ − __3__ − __1__ = ?

__10__ − __1__ = __9__

14 − 5 = ?

_____ − _____ − _____ = ?

_____ − _____ = _____

15 − 7 = ?

_____ − _____ − _____ = ?

_____ − _____ = _____

16 − 9 = ?

_____ − _____ − _____ = ?

_____ − _____ = _____

14 − 6 = ?

_____ − _____ − _____ = ?

_____ − _____ = _____

17 − 8 = ?

_____ − _____ − _____ = ?

_____ − _____ = _____

Subtract. Make a 10 to help!

13 − 5 = _____

14 − 5 = _____

13 − 7 = _____

15 − 6 = _____

14 − 9 = _____

12 − 5 = _____

14 − 6 = _____

17 − 8 = _____

12 − 4 = _____

15 − 9 = _____

16 − 9 = _____

12 − 8 = _____

17 − 9 = _____

16 − 7 = _____

15 − 7 = _____

14 − 8 = _____

Time to review! Add or subtract.

$16 - 5 =$ _____

$7 + 7 =$ _____

$6 + 4 =$ _____

$11 - 6 =$ _____

$8 + 7 =$ _____

$5 + 9 =$ _____

$17 - 8 =$ _____

$12 - 6 =$ _____

$13 - 5 =$ _____

$7 + 4 =$ _____

$4 + 8 =$ _____

$15 - 7 =$ _____

$14 - 6 =$ _____

$9 + 9 =$ _____

IXL.com
skill ID
QQP

Add or subtract.

5 + 8 = _____   9 + 3 = _____

12 − 7 = _____   13 − 4 = _____

16 − 9 = _____   2 + 8 = _____

3 + 7 = _____   15 − 6 = _____

17 − 7 = _____   12 − 8 = _____

13 − 2 = _____   8 + 6 = _____

11 − 8 = _____   8 + 8 = _____

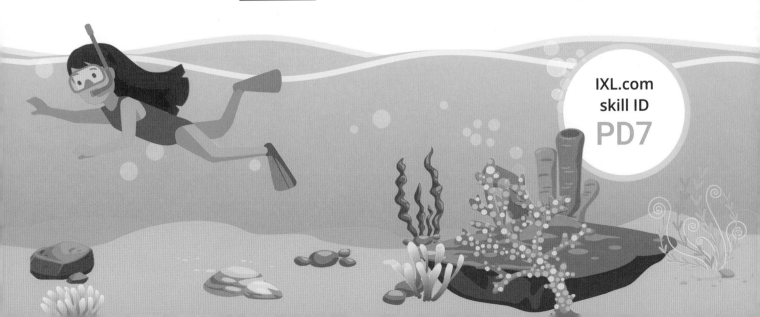

IXL.com
skill ID
PD7

Add or subtract. Draw a line between the matching answers.

3 + 4 = 7   5 + 4

12 − 3   6 + 9

6 + 4   14 − 7 = 7

7 + 8   2 + 8

9 + 5   12 − 6

5 + 8   6 + 8

10 − 6   15 − 7

9 − 3   7 + 6

6 + 2   13 − 9

IXL.com
skill ID
F99

Fill in the boxes to complete each puzzle.

Puzzle 1 (top left):

START

2 → +6 → 8

↓ −2

9 ← +3 ← 6

FINISH

Puzzle 2 (top right):

☐ → +4 → ☐

↑ −5 ↓ −3

12 ☐

START FINISH

Puzzle 3 (bottom left):

FINISH START

☐ 14

↑ −8 ↓ −5

☐ ← +7 ← ☐

Puzzle 4 (bottom right):

FINISH

☐ → −9 → ☐

↑ +7

☐ ← −4 ← 12

START

IXL.com
skill ID
KP6

Kathleen goes to Game World with her family. The poster shows how many coins each game costs to play.

Game World

Eat 'em Up . . . . 2 coins

Space Racers . . . . 4 coins

Bop the Bullseye . . . . 5 coins

Answer each question.

Kathleen plays Eat 'em Up. Then she plays Space Racers. How many coins does she use?

_____ coins

Kathleen started with 15 coins. How many does she have left after she plays Eat 'em Up and Space Racers?

_____ coins

Kathleen uses 6 more coins playing other games. After that, she wants to play Bop the Bullseye. Does she have enough coins to play?

_____

Kathleen wins tickets for each game she plays. She can use her tickets to get prizes.

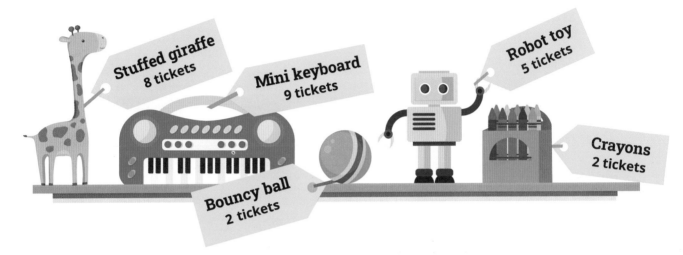

Stuffed giraffe
8 tickets

Mini keyboard
9 tickets

Robot toy
5 tickets

Crayons
2 tickets

Bouncy ball
2 tickets

Answer each question.

Kathleen has 16 tickets. Then she buys the stuffed giraffe. How many tickets does she have left?

_____ tickets

Kathleen wants to buy the robot toy and the mini keyboard. How many tickets does she need?

_____ tickets

Kathleen and her brother decide to buy the robot toy and the mini keyboard together. Kathleen uses 6 tickets. How many tickets does her brother use?

_____ tickets

IXL.com
skill ID
75R

You can use number lines to help you add with larger numbers.
Try it yourself! Fill in the blanks to add.

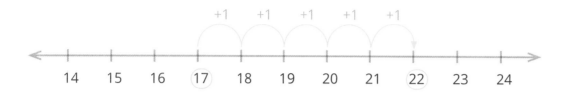

__17__ + __5__ = __22__

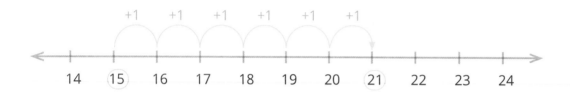

_____ + _____ = _____

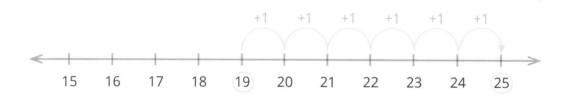

_____ + _____ = _____

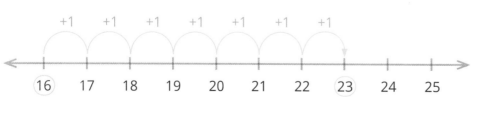

_____ + _____ = _____

IXL.com
skill ID
FXF

Add.

18 + 4 = _____

20 + 4 = _____

14 + 6 = _____

19 + 2 = _____

17 + 7 = _____

16 + 5 = _____

18 + 5 = _____

19 + 4 = _____

16 + 4 = _____

13 + 9 = _____

19 + 6 = _____

22 + 3 = _____

17 + 6 = _____

18 + 6 = _____

Let's Learn!

When you add more than two numbers, you can group the numbers in any way! Try it for 8 + 8 + 3. You can start by adding 8 + 8. Or, you can start by adding 8 + 3.

$$8 + 8 + 3$$
$$\vee$$
$$16 + 3 = 19$$

$$8 + 8 + 3$$
$$\vee$$
$$8 + 11 = 19$$

Group the numbers in two ways to add.

$(6 + 4) + 7 = \underline{10} + \underline{7} = \underline{17}$ $1 + 9 + 8 = \underline{} + \underline{} = \underline{}$

$6 + (4 + 7) = \underline{6} + \underline{11} = \underline{17}$ $1 + 9 + 8 = \underline{} + \underline{} = \underline{}$

$6 + 6 + 5 = \underline{} + \underline{} = \underline{}$ $8 + 7 + 9 = \underline{} + \underline{} = \underline{}$

$6 + 6 + 5 = \underline{} + \underline{} = \underline{}$ $8 + 7 + 9 = \underline{} + \underline{} = \underline{}$

$9 + 9 + 5 = \underline{} + \underline{} = \underline{}$ $5 + 8 + 8 = \underline{} + \underline{} = \underline{}$

$9 + 9 + 5 = \underline{} + \underline{} = \underline{}$ $5 + 8 + 8 = \underline{} + \underline{} = \underline{}$

TAKE ANOTHER LOOK! Which way was easier to add? Write a check mark next to the easier problem in each pair.

Add.

3 + 7 + 7 = _____   3 + 5 + 4 = _____

8 + 4 + 3 = _____   6 + 4 + 2 = _____

7 + 3 + 2 = _____   6 + 6 + 4 = _____

9 + 3 + 7 = _____   5 + 7 + 4 = _____

4 + 8 + 8 = _____   2 + 8 + 9 = _____

9 + 4 + 9 = _____   6 + 8 + 7 = _____

3 + 8 + 7 = _____   8 + 9 + 5 = _____

IXL.com
skill ID
YCC

Add.

4 + 4 + 8 + 2 = _____   6 + 2 + 7 + 3 = _____

3 + 8 + 7 + 7 = _____   1 + 9 + 7 + 5 = _____

6 + 2 + 8 + 5 = _____   9 + 6 + 5 + 5 = _____

7 + 2 + 9 + 3 = _____   9 + 3 + 1 + 2 = _____

8 + 3 + 5 + 6 = _____   6 + 6 + 5 + 2 = _____

3 + 6 + 4 + 3 = _____   4 + 6 + 8 + 7 = _____

IXL.com
skill ID
77J

Each puzzle uses the numbers 1–9 once. If you add across, you get the number on the right. If you add down, you get the number on the bottom. Fill in the missing numbers.

Puzzle 1:

7	9	2	18
3	4	1	8
8	6	5	19
18	19	8	

Puzzle 2:

1			17
	4		13
5		2	15
9	21	15	

Puzzle 3:

9	8		19
	4	3	14
			12
22	17	6	

Puzzle 4:

	4	2	15
	6	3	17
			13
18	17	10	

Answer each question.

Annie is counting the flowers she sees on a walk. She counts 4 red flowers, 8 white flowers, and 5 purple flowers. How many flowers does Annie see in all?

_____ flowers

Nick made a list of the people who are coming to his birthday party. He wrote down the names of 6 friends from his basketball team. He also wrote down 8 friends from school and 5 neighbors. How many people are coming to his party?

_____ people

Raina is counting the fish in her friend's fish tank. She counts 3 blue fish, 8 red fish, and 5 yellow fish. How many fish does Raina count in all?

_____ fish

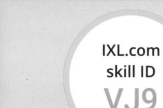

IXL.com
skill ID
VJ9

Let's Learn!

Adding the same number many times is called **repeated addition**. You can use repeated addition to add equal groups.

Look at this example. If you have 3 groups of 4 ducks, the total is 4 + 4 + 4 = 12 ducks.

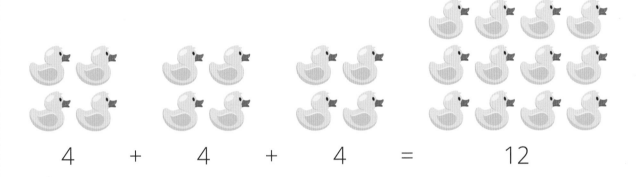

4 + 4 + 4 = 12

Add.

2 + 2 + 2 = _____

5 + 5 + 5 = _____

6 + 6 + 6 = _____

3 + 3 + 3 = _____

8 + 8 + 8 = _____

7 + 7 + 7 = _____

10 + 10 + 10 = _____

9 + 9 + 9 = _____

You can use repeated addition for rows of things, too!

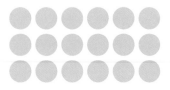 3 rows

For example, here are 3 rows of 2 dots.
There are 6 dots because 2 + 2 + 2 = 6.

Fill in the blanks. Add the rows.

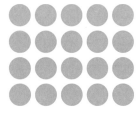

$$\underline{6} + \underline{6} + \underline{6} = \underline{18}$$

$$\underline{} + \underline{} + \underline{} + \underline{} = \underline{}$$

$$\underline{} + \underline{} + \underline{} + \underline{} = \underline{}$$

Fill in the blanks. Add the rows.

_____ + _____ + _____ = _____

_____ + _____ + _____ + _____ = _____

_____ + _____ + _____ + _____ = _____

_____ + _____ + _____ = _____

Mr. Gibson is a farmer. Help him count his crops. Use repeated addition to find each total.

_____ ears of corn

_____ heads of broccoli

_____ tomatoes

_____ pumpkins

Answer each question about Mr. Gibson's farm.

Mr. Gibson has 10 cows with black spots and 10 cows with brown spots. How many cows does he have in all?

_____ cows

The farm has 3 barns. Each barn holds 6 horses. How many horses are there in all?

_____ horses

Mr. Gibson has 5 brown goats, 5 white goats, and 5 black goats. How many goats does he have in all?

_____ goats

Mr. Gibson's fence is broken in 3 places. He needs 7 pieces of wood to fix each place. How many pieces of wood does Mr. Gibson need to fix his fence?

_____ pieces of wood

The tractors and trucks on the farm need new tires. Mr. Gibson bought 8 new tractor tires and 8 new truck tires. How many tires did he buy?

_____ tires

Exploration Zone

MULTIPLICATION

If you have equal groups or equal rows, you can use multiplication instead of repeated addition! See how it works for these 3 groups of 8 crayons. The × symbol shows multiplication.

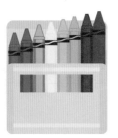  

8 + 8 + 8 = 24 crayons

3 × 8 = 24 crayons

IXL.com
skill ID
LN5

TRY IT YOURSELF!

There are 3 groups of 2 mittens. How many mittens are there in all?

_3_ × _2_ = _6_ mittens

There are 5 groups of 2 toothbrushes. How many toothbrushes are there in all?

_____ × _____ = _____ toothbrushes

A muffin pan holds 3 rows of 4 muffins. How many muffins does the pan hold?

_____ × _____ = _____ muffins

A parking lot has 2 rows of 4 cars. How many cars are parked in the parking lot?

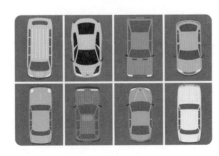

_____ × _____ = _____ cars

Let's Learn!

You can use blocks to add larger numbers. For example, try it with 31 + 7. Count the blocks.

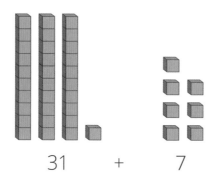

31 + 7

There are 3 tens blocks and 8 ones blocks, so 31 + 7 = 38.

Add.

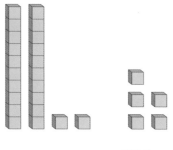

22 + 5 = __27__

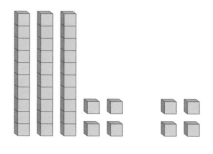

34 + 4 = _____

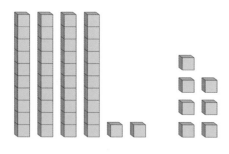

42 + 7 = _____

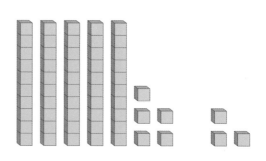

55 + 3 = _____

Add.

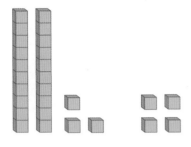

23 + 4 = _____

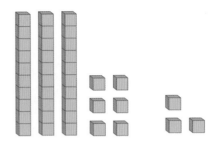

36 + 3 = _____

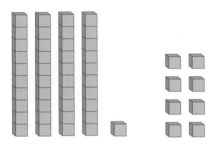

41 + 8 = _____

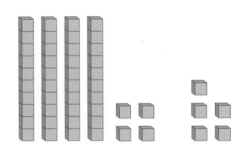

44 + 5 = _____

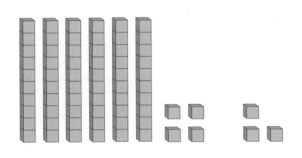

64 + 3 = _____

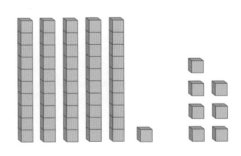

51 + 7 = _____

For more practice, visit IXL.com or the IXL mobile app and enter this code in the search bar.

IXL.com
skill ID
QC9

Add. Think about blocks to help.

37 + 2 = _____   23 + 6 = _____

24 + 5 = _____   31 + 7 = _____

42 + 3 = _____   28 + 1 = _____

56 + 2 = _____   41 + 5 = _____

64 + 4 = _____   53 + 4 = _____

72 + 6 = _____   86 + 3 = _____

IXL.com
skill ID
EZ7

Keep going with larger numbers! Add.

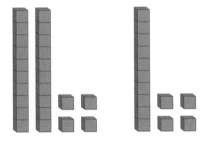

32 + 25 = __57__

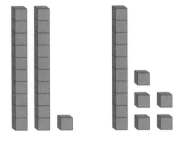

21 + 15 = _____

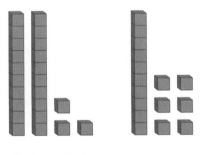

24 + 14 = _____

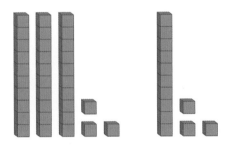

33 + 13 = _____

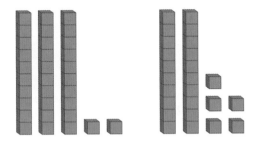

23 + 16 = _____

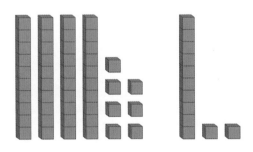

47 + 12 = _____

Add.

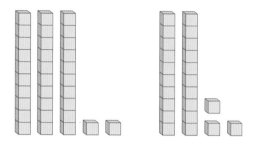

32 + 23 = _____

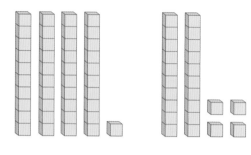

41 + 24 = _____

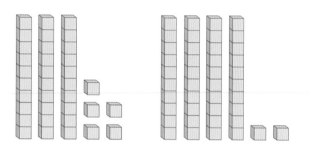

35 + 42 = _____

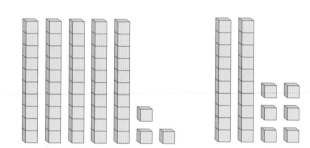

53 + 26 = _____

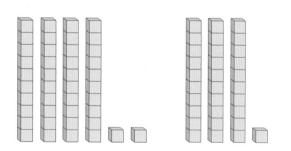

42 + 31 = _____

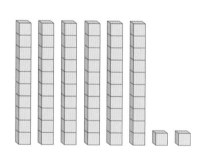

62 + 22 = _____

IXL.com
skill ID
GK2

Add. Think about blocks to help.

12 + 14 = _____   34 + 13 = _____

23 + 25 = _____   17 + 22 = _____

36 + 23 = _____   43 + 24 = _____

32 + 21 = _____   31 + 48 = _____

33 + 52 = _____   42 + 46 = _____

54 + 35 = _____   56 + 22 = _____

67 + 11 = _____   54 + 45 = _____

Let's Learn!

You can make a ten to solve harder addition problems. Try it with 47 + 6. Move 3 of the ones blocks to make 50. There are 3 ones blocks left.

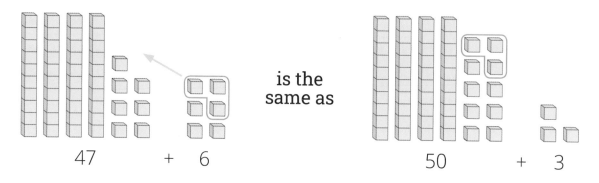

47 + 6   is the same as   50 + 3

As you can see, 47 + 6 is the same as 50 + 3. So, the sum is 53!

Move the ones blocks to make a ten. Then fill in the blanks to add.

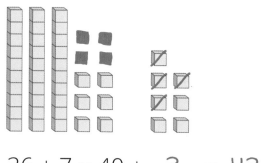

36 + 7 = 40 + _3_ = _43_

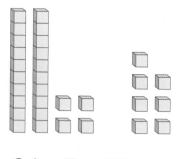

24 + 7 = 30 + ____ = ____

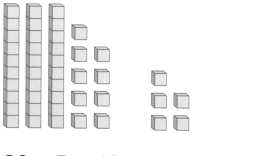

39 + 5 = 40 + ____ = ____

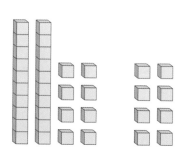

28 + 8 = 30 + ____ = ____

Fill in the blanks to add.

56 + 9 = 60 + _5_ = _65_   26 + 5 = 30 + ____ = ____

38 + 4 = 40 + ____ = ____   47 + 7 = 50 + ____ = ____

76 + 8 = 80 + ____ = ____   33 + 9 = 40 + ____ = ____

65 + 6 = 70 + ____ = ____   54 + 8 = 60 + ____ = ____

Add. Make tens to help.

49 + 4 = _____   78 + 5 = _____

32 + 9 = _____   26 + 6 = _____

67 + 5 = _____   53 + 8 = _____

88 + 3 = _____   75 + 9 = _____

IXL.com
skill ID
8BT

Let's Learn!

You can use place value to add. For example, try it with 24 + 33.

$$\begin{array}{r} 2\,4 \\ +\ 3\,3 \\ \hline 7 \end{array}$$

4 + 3 = 7

First, line up the numbers.

Then, add the **ones**. Write the sum below the line.

$$\begin{array}{r} 2\,4 \\ +\ 3\,3 \\ \hline 5\,7 \end{array}$$

2 + 3 = 5

Now, add the **tens**. Write the sum below the line.

The number below the line is the answer! So, 24 + 33 = 57.

Add.

$$\begin{array}{r} 4\,5 \\ +\ 2\,3 \\ \hline 6\,8 \end{array}$$

$$\begin{array}{r} 2\,2 \\ +\ 6\,5 \\ \hline \end{array}$$

$$\begin{array}{r} 7\,2 \\ +\ 2\,1 \\ \hline \end{array}$$

$$\begin{array}{r} 3\,1 \\ +\ 4\,8 \\ \hline \end{array}$$

$$\begin{array}{r} 2\,4 \\ +\ 2\,4 \\ \hline \end{array}$$

$$\begin{array}{r} 3\,3 \\ +\ 4\,4 \\ \hline \end{array}$$

Add.

23 +35	37 +12	32 +34
42 +22	51 +38	42 +42
73 +24	12 +71	43 +36
84 +14	15 +41	24 +63
33 +32	64 +35	62 +16
32 +62	55 +43	

IXL.com
skill ID
TX5

Let's Learn!

Sometimes you need to regroup when you add. For example, try it with 35 + 27.

$$
\begin{array}{r}
{}^{1}\,3\,5 \\
+\,2\,7 \\
\hline
2
\end{array}
$$

5 + 7 = 12

First, line up the numbers.

Add the **ones**. The sum is 12, which doesn't fit below the ones.

Remember that 12 is the same as 1 ten and 2 ones. Put the 2 in the ones column, and move the 1 to the tens column.

$$
\begin{array}{r}
{}^{1}\,3\,5 \\
+\,2\,7 \\
\hline
6\,2
\end{array}
$$

1 + 3 + 2 = 6

Now, add all the **tens**. Write the sum below the line.

The number below the line is the answer! So, 35 + 27 = 62.

Add.

$$
\begin{array}{r}
{}^{1}\,4\,6 \\
+\,3\,5 \\
\hline
8\,1
\end{array}
\qquad
\begin{array}{r}
2\,8 \\
+\,1\,4 \\
\hline
\end{array}
\qquad
\begin{array}{r}
1\,9 \\
+\,3\,6 \\
\hline
\end{array}
$$

$$
\begin{array}{r}
3\,3 \\
+\,5\,7 \\
\hline
\end{array}
\qquad
\begin{array}{r}
5\,9 \\
+\,3\,9 \\
\hline
\end{array}
\qquad
\begin{array}{r}
4\,8 \\
+\,3\,6 \\
\hline
\end{array}
$$

Add.

$$
\begin{array}{r} 2\,6 \\ +\,1\,7 \\ \hline \end{array}
\qquad
\begin{array}{r} 2\,4 \\ +\,3\,8 \\ \hline \end{array}
\qquad
\begin{array}{r} 6\,5 \\ +\,2\,7 \\ \hline \end{array}
$$

$$
\begin{array}{r} 3\,9 \\ +\,4\,1 \\ \hline \end{array}
\qquad
\begin{array}{r} 7\,7 \\ +\,1\,6 \\ \hline \end{array}
\qquad
\begin{array}{r} 3\,8 \\ +\,2\,9 \\ \hline \end{array}
$$

$$
\begin{array}{r} 7\,9 \\ +\,1\,2 \\ \hline \end{array}
\qquad
\begin{array}{r} 3\,2 \\ +\,1\,9 \\ \hline \end{array}
\qquad
\begin{array}{r} 5\,6 \\ +\,2\,6 \\ \hline \end{array}
$$

$$
\begin{array}{r} 6\,8 \\ +\,2\,7 \\ \hline \end{array}
\qquad
\begin{array}{r} 2\,7 \\ +\,4\,7 \\ \hline \end{array}
\qquad
\begin{array}{r} 7\,9 \\ +\,1\,5 \\ \hline \end{array}
$$

IXL.com
skill ID
GLX

Add.

```
  2 7        4 2        3 8
+ 4 5      + 3 6      + 3 3
```

```
  5 2        2 6        3 9
+ 4 7      + 6 4      + 1 4
```

```
  5 3        4 8        3 5
+ 2 4      + 4 8      + 3 6
```

```
  6 4        2 6        5 4
+ 2 7      + 3 9      + 2 2
```

```
  3 6        1 8        7 1
+ 4 3      + 6 4      + 2 5
```

IXL.com
skill ID
GZY

Add. Compare the answers in each row. Circle the largest one.

```
   49          28          26
 + 16        + 36        + 52
```

```
   54          48          39
 + 24        + 33        + 19
```

```
   29          23          36
 + 44        + 52        + 35
```

```
   37          14          28
 + 54        + 76        + 58
```

```
   16          27          18
 + 63        + 49        + 62
```

IXL.com
skill ID
CZK

Write the missing numbers. Each number in the pyramid is the sum of the two numbers below it.

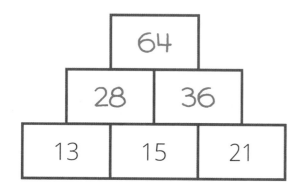

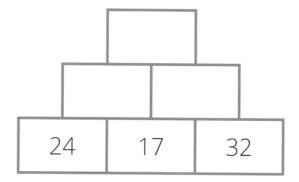

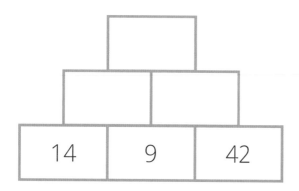

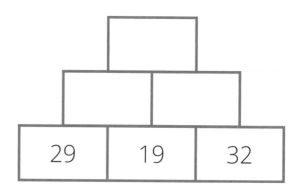

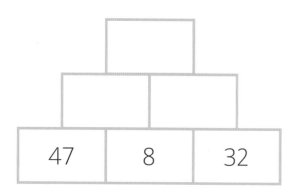

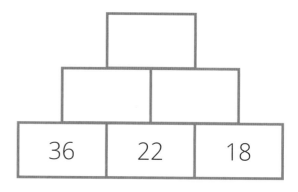

Follow the path!

If the sum is less than 50, move one square to the left.

If the sum is between 50 and 80, move one square down.

If the sum is greater than 80, move one square to the right.

START

55 +28	68 +26	21 +40	39 +48	57 +17
44 +15	14 +28	24 +17	57 +25	29 +29
36 +16	44 +55	63 +21	45 +38	46 +22
59 +39	46 +43	65 +27	57 +22	62 +19
74 +19	29 +35	59 +20	81 +13	44 +28

FINISH

Answer each question.

Brady and Noah are building towers with blocks. Brady uses 36 blocks to build his tower. Noah uses 25 more blocks than Brady to build his tower. How many blocks does Noah use?

_____ blocks

There are 27 children in Mia's class. A different class joins Mia's class to play four corners. The other class has 21 children. How many children in all are playing four corners?

_____ children

Sasha's house is 38 minutes from her grandmother's house. How many minutes would it take to go to her grandmother's house and back?

_____ minutes

Devon and his dad finished 2 jigsaw puzzles. The first puzzle had 48 pieces. The second puzzle had 24 pieces. How many pieces is that in all?

_____ pieces

Sam and his dad are going to Monster Land Theme Park. Answer each question.

Sam's dad buys one Big Monster ticket and one Small Monster ticket. How much does he pay?

TICKET PRICES:

BIG MONSTERS (ADULTS) $48

SMALL MONSTERS (KIDS) $29

_____

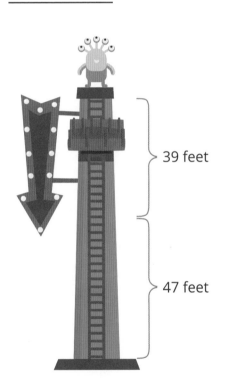

39 feet

47 feet

The Super Slinger is Sam's favorite ride. It brings riders 47 feet in the air and spins them around. Then it goes up another 39 feet to the top. How far up in the air do Super Slinger riders go?

_____ feet

Sam's dad likes the Monster Mountain ride. Riders take a train up and around Monster Mountain. Each train can hold 26 riders. If there are 2 trains, how many riders can ride Monster Mountain at once?

_____ riders

IXL.com skill ID

XAT

Let's Learn!

You can use blocks to subtract larger numbers. Try it with 48 − 5.

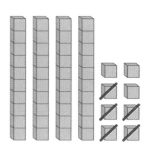

Use 4 tens blocks and 8 ones blocks to show 48.

Subtract 5 by crossing out 5 of the ones blocks.

Count how many blocks are left. There are 4 tens blocks and 3 ones blocks.

So, 48 − 5 = 43.

Cross out blocks to subtract.

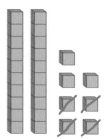

27 − 4 = ___23___

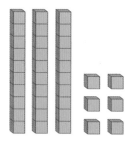

36 − 6 = _____

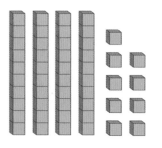

49 − 8 = _____

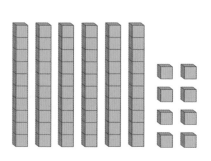

68 − 5 = _____

Cross out blocks to subtract.

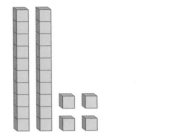

24 – 2 = _____

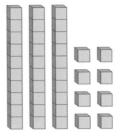

38 – 3 = _____

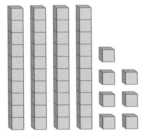

47 – 5 = _____

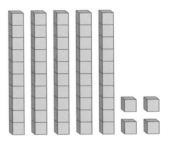

54 – 4 = _____

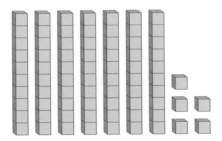

75 – 4 = _____

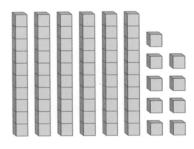

69 – 7 = _____

Subtract. Think about blocks to help.

25 − 4 = _____

36 − 3 = _____

44 − 2 = _____

38 − 1 = _____

59 − 5 = _____

47 − 6 = _____

67 − 7 = _____

54 − 3 = _____

89 − 8 = _____

72 − 2 = _____

IXL.com
skill ID
L8D

Let's Learn!

You can use blocks to subtract even larger numbers! Try it with 65 − 12.

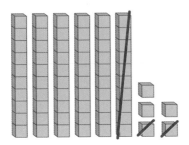

Use 6 tens blocks and 5 ones blocks to show 65.

Since 12 is the same as 1 ten and 2 ones, cross out 1 tens block and 2 ones blocks.

Count how many blocks are left. There are 5 tens blocks and 3 ones blocks.

So, 65 − 12 = 53.

Cross out blocks to subtract.

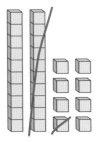

28 − 11 = ___17___

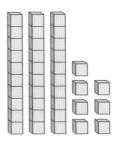

37 − 22 = _____

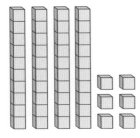

46 − 16 = _____

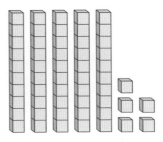

55 − 34 = _____

Cross out blocks to subtract.

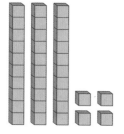

34 − 11 = _____

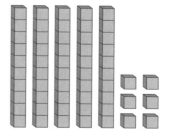

56 − 35 = _____

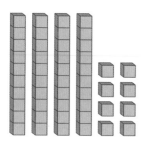

48 − 24 = _____

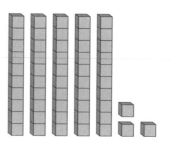

53 − 12 = _____

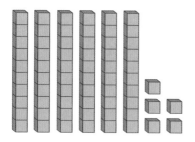

65 − 15 = _____

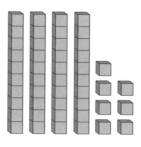

47 − 34 = _____

Subtract. Think about blocks to help.

34 − 21 = _____

39 − 15 = _____

63 − 22 = _____

79 − 43 = _____

58 − 41 = _____

37 − 25 = _____

49 − 27 = _____

56 − 34 = _____

67 − 32 = _____

73 − 31 = _____

Let's Learn!

Sometimes you need to regroup the tens and ones to subtract.
Try it with 54 − 9.

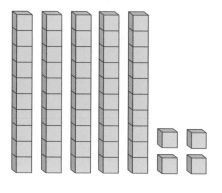

Use 5 tens blocks and 4 ones blocks to show 54. You need to cross out 9 ones. But there are only 4 ones blocks!

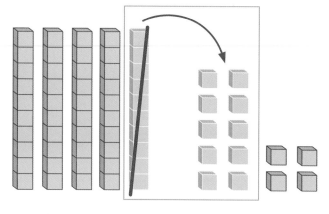

Remember, a ten is made of ten ones. Take one tens block and split it into ones.

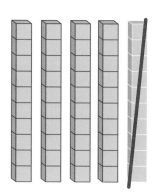 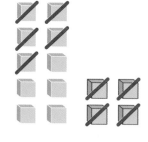

Now, you have 14 ones blocks. You can cross out 9! There are 4 tens blocks and 5 ones blocks left.

So, 54 − 9 = 45.

Regroup. Then cross out blocks to subtract.

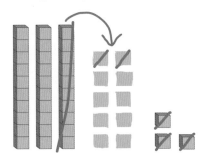

33 − 5 = __28__

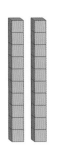

24 − 8 = _____

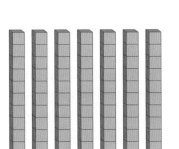

73 − 4 = _____

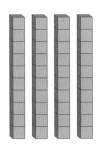

42 − 7 = _____

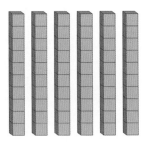

66 − 9 = _____

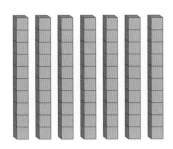

71 − 6 = _____

IXL.com
skill ID
P85

Let's Learn!

You can use place value to subtract. For example, try it with 36 – 15.

$$\begin{array}{r} 3\,6 \\ -\,1\,5 \\ \hline 1 \end{array}$$

6 – 5 = 1

First, line up the numbers.

Then, subtract the **ones**. Write the difference below the line.

$$\begin{array}{r} 3\,6 \\ -\,1\,5 \\ \hline 2\,1 \end{array}$$

3 – 1 = 2

Now, subtract the **tens**. Write the difference below the line.

The number below the line is the answer! So, 36 – 15 = 21.

Subtract.

$$\begin{array}{r} 4\,5 \\ -\,2\,3 \\ \hline 2\,2 \end{array}$$

$$\begin{array}{r} 5\,4 \\ -\,1\,3 \\ \hline \end{array}$$

$$\begin{array}{r} 6\,3 \\ -\,3\,1 \\ \hline \end{array}$$

$$\begin{array}{r} 6\,8 \\ -\,2\,1 \\ \hline \end{array}$$

$$\begin{array}{r} 7\,5 \\ -\,3\,2 \\ \hline \end{array}$$

$$\begin{array}{r} 4\,8 \\ -\,1\,7 \\ \hline \end{array}$$

Subtract.

$$\begin{array}{r} 4\ 8 \\ -\ 2\ 3 \\ \hline \end{array}$$

$$\begin{array}{r} 5\ 6 \\ -\ 1\ 2 \\ \hline \end{array}$$

$$\begin{array}{r} 3\ 3 \\ -\ 2\ 2 \\ \hline \end{array}$$

$$\begin{array}{r} 6\ 5 \\ -\ 3\ 4 \\ \hline \end{array}$$

$$\begin{array}{r} 4\ 7 \\ -\ 2\ 4 \\ \hline \end{array}$$

$$\begin{array}{r} 5\ 9 \\ -\ 2\ 7 \\ \hline \end{array}$$

$$\begin{array}{r} 7\ 8 \\ -\ 4\ 1 \\ \hline \end{array}$$

$$\begin{array}{r} 6\ 9 \\ -\ 5\ 4 \\ \hline \end{array}$$

$$\begin{array}{r} 4\ 6 \\ -\ 3\ 3 \\ \hline \end{array}$$

$$\begin{array}{r} 8\ 4 \\ -\ 1\ 3 \\ \hline \end{array}$$

$$\begin{array}{r} 5\ 2 \\ -\ 2\ 1 \\ \hline \end{array}$$

$$\begin{array}{r} 8\ 5 \\ -\ 5\ 2 \\ \hline \end{array}$$

$$\begin{array}{r} 9\ 7 \\ -\ 5\ 6 \\ \hline \end{array}$$

$$\begin{array}{r} 6\ 7 \\ -\ 4\ 1 \\ \hline \end{array}$$

$$\begin{array}{r} 6\ 8 \\ -\ 4\ 5 \\ \hline \end{array}$$

$$\begin{array}{r} 9\ 6 \\ -\ 4\ 2 \\ \hline \end{array}$$

$$\begin{array}{r} 3\ 9 \\ -\ 2\ 3 \\ \hline \end{array}$$

IXL.com
skill ID
R8C

Let's Learn!

Sometimes, you need to regroup to subtract. For example, try it with 42 − 27.

$$\begin{array}{r} 3\,\overset{\frown}{12} \\ \cancel{4}\,2 \\ -\ 2\,7 \\ \hline 5 \end{array}$$

First, line up the numbers.

Try to subtract the **ones**. You can't do 2 − 7! You need to borrow from the tens.

Remember that 42 is the same as 30 + 12. Cross out the 4 and write 3. Cross out the 2 and write 12. Now you can subtract.

$$\begin{array}{r} \overset{\frown}{3}\ 12 \\ \cancel{4}\,2 \\ -\ 2\,7 \\ \hline 1\,5 \end{array}$$

Next, subtract the **tens**.

The number below the line is the answer.
So, 42 − 27 = 15!

Subtract.

$$\begin{array}{r} {}^{4}\ {}^{15} \\ \cancel{5}\,\cancel{5} \\ -\ 1\,8 \\ \hline 3\,7 \end{array} \qquad \begin{array}{r} 3\,8 \\ -\ 1\,9 \\ \hline \end{array} \qquad \begin{array}{r} 4\,5 \\ -\ 2\,8 \\ \hline \end{array}$$

$$\begin{array}{r} 6\,2 \\ -\ 3\,5 \\ \hline \end{array} \qquad \begin{array}{r} 7\,3 \\ -\ 2\,7 \\ \hline \end{array} \qquad \begin{array}{r} 8\,4 \\ -\ 3\,9 \\ \hline \end{array}$$

Subtract.

```
   6 3          8 6          7 5
 - 2 6        - 5 7        - 6 7
```

```
   4 2          7 4          5 6
 - 2 4        - 3 8        - 2 8
```

```
   8 2          9 2          8 0
 - 4 5        - 6 7        - 4 7
```

```
   4 1          8 7          5 0
 - 1 8        - 4 9        - 3 6
```

IXL.com
skill ID
TWE

Subtract. Compare the answers in each row. Circle the smallest one.

29 − 1 8	3 5 − 2 2	4 2 − 3 4
7 4 − 5 8	5 6 − 2 5	6 7 − 3 9
4 9 − 2 9	7 0 − 4 2	8 4 − 5 5
9 8 − 6 9	6 4 − 3 8	5 6 − 2 7
7 6 − 2 7	8 5 − 3 2	5 7 − 1 9

Fill in the missing digits.

$$\begin{array}{r} \boxed{7}\,6 \\ -\ 3\ 1 \\ \hline 4\ 5 \end{array}$$

$$\begin{array}{r} 8\ 4 \\ -\ \boxed{\ }\ 3 \\ \hline 2\ 1 \end{array}$$

$$\begin{array}{r} 7\ 6 \\ -\ 3\ \boxed{\ } \\ \hline 4\ 4 \end{array}$$

$$\begin{array}{r} 8\ 6 \\ -\ 4\ \boxed{\ } \\ \hline 3\ 7 \end{array}$$

$$\begin{array}{r} \boxed{\ }\ 9 \\ -\ 5\ 4 \\ \hline 3\ 5 \end{array}$$

$$\begin{array}{r} 8\ \boxed{\ } \\ -\ 4\ 3 \\ \hline 3\ 9 \end{array}$$

$$\begin{array}{r} 9\ 7 \\ -\ \boxed{\ }\ 8 \\ \hline 2\ 9 \end{array}$$

$$\begin{array}{r} 4\ \boxed{\ } \\ -\ 1\ 7 \\ \hline 2\ 3 \end{array}$$

$$\begin{array}{r} 6\ 6 \\ -\ 1\ \boxed{\ } \\ \hline 4\ 8 \end{array}$$

IXL.com
skill ID
YWC

Answer each question.

Wendy played at the park for 54 minutes. Kendra played at the park for 67 minutes. How much longer did Kendra play at the park than Wendy?

_____ minutes

James is playing basketball. He shot the basketball 37 times. He missed 15 of those shots. How many shots went in?

_____ shots

Milo has $39. His brother, Parker, has $83. How much more money does Parker have than Milo?

_____

Jason's soccer team is having a bake sale. There are 70 baked goods for sale. After the bake sale, there are 13 baked goods left over. How many baked goods did Jason's team sell?

_____ baked goods

IXL.com
skill ID
UFU

Each morning, the campers at Sunny Cove Summer Camp sign up for an afternoon activity.

Answer each question about the activities.

How many more campers signed up for rock climbing than boating?

_____ campers

How many more campers signed up for swimming than boating?

_____ campers

There are two different rock walls for rock climbing.

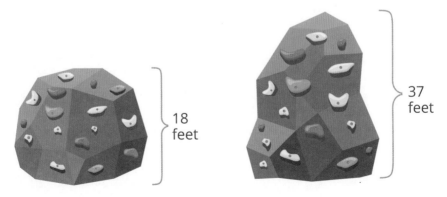

18 feet

37 feet

How much taller is the big wall than the small wall?

_____ feet

Let's review! Add or subtract.

```
  6 5          4 8          7 8
+ 2 3        - 2 3        - 3 6
```

```
  3 6          8 3          3 3
+ 4 1        - 2 7        + 3 4
```

```
  4 2          6 7          5 7
- 2 5        - 1 8        + 2 3
```

```
  9 1          2 5          5 3
- 3 8        + 5 7        + 3 8
```

Find the row, column, or diagonal line where all the sums and differences are the same.

34 +39 **73**	61 +12 **73**	92 −19 **73**
95 −22 **73**	64 +12 **76**	83 −16 **67**
83 −20 **63**	32 +51 **83**	79 −26 **53**

97 −38	43 +16	32 +25
27 +31	83 −24	29 +28
72 −23	17 +42	70 −21

29 +53	91 −25	39 +27
92 −25	94 −12	19 +48
87 −29	75 −17	49 +33

39 +29	82 −14	55 +12
90 −23	27 +42	95 −28
27 +41	87 −19	49 +19

IXL.com
skill ID
JDT

Answer each question.

Jack's Ice Cream Shop has 27 flavors. For a contest, the shop makes 15 new flavors. How many flavors does the shop have now?

_____ flavors

Levi is trying to guess how many candies are in a jar. He guesses that there are 58 candies. There are 72 candies in the jar. How far off was his guess?

_____ candies

Casey and Mason are playing a board game. On Casey's first turn, she moved 12 jumps. On her second turn, she moved 19 jumps. How many jumps did she move in her first two turns?

_____ jumps

Ashley has 63 building blocks. She uses 45 blocks to make a castle. How many blocks are left over?

_____ blocks

Let's Learn!

Rule: subtract 8	
In	**Out**
19 – 8 11	
38 – 8 30	
57 – 8 49	

This table is called an **input/output table**. It takes numbers **in** and then puts new numbers **out** based on a rule.

For example, this table's rule is subtract 8. If you put in 19, you **subtract 8** to get 11.

Complete each input/output table.

Rule: add 26	
In	**Out**
22	48
35	61
57	83

Rule: subtract 23	
In	**Out**
35	12
54	
62	39

Rule: add 54	
In	**Out**
14	68
27	
36	90

Rule: subtract 37	
In	**Out**
43	
51	14
79	42

Complete each input/output table.

Rule: add 21	
In	**Out**
19	
30	51
57	

Rule: subtract 29	
In	**Out**
35	6
59	
77	

Rule: subtract 25	
In	**Out**
32	
49	24
66	

Rule: add 28	
In	**Out**
17	
26	54
38	

Rule: subtract 59	
In	**Out**
61	2
72	
84	

IXL.com
skill ID
6XK

Find the rule for each input/output table.

In	Out
25	59
33	67
45	79

Rule: ___ADD 34___

In	Out
32	18
55	41
68	54

Rule: _____

In	Out
56	19
66	29
70	33

Rule: _____

In	Out
28	54
56	82
61	87

Rule: _____

In	Out
13	87
19	93
22	96

Rule: _____

IXL.com
skill ID
LXX

Let's Learn!

Numbers can be **even** or **odd**.

Even numbers can be matched in pairs. For example, 8 is an even number.

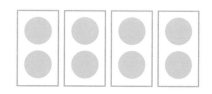

Odd numbers cannot be matched in pairs. For example, 5 is an odd number. There is one left over with no match.

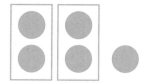

Answer each question.

Is 4 even or odd? _____

Is 9 even or odd? _____

Is 17 even or odd? _____

Is 20 even or odd? _____

Circle all the even numbers.

7	2	1	10
13	6	3	15

IXL.com
skill ID
54Z

Let's Learn!

You can tell if a number is even by looking at the **ones place**. Skip count by 2s to see how.

2   4   6   8   10

12   14   16   18   20

22   24   26   28   30

These numbers are all even. The ones place for each number has a 0, 2, 4, 6, or 8.

Any number with a 0, 2, 4, 6, or 8 in the ones place is even. All other numbers are odd!

Circle the ones place. Then write even or odd.

4(3) ___ODD___   5 6 _____

7 0 _____   6 4 _____

2 7 _____   9 1 _____

1 2 9 _____   2 1 2 _____

6 5 8 _____   9 4 5 _____

IXL.com
skill ID
JLX

ADDING EVENS AND ODDS

Will the answer to an addition problem be even or odd? You can tell by looking at the numbers you are adding! See if you can find the pattern below.

$3 + 4 = 7$

<u>ODD</u> + <u>EVEN</u> = <u>ODD</u>

$6 + 8 = 14$

_____ + _____ = _____

$9 + 3 = 12$

_____ + _____ = _____

$10 + 7 = 17$

_____ + _____ = _____

$2 + 8 = 10$

_____ + _____ = _____

$3 + 13 = 16$

_____ + _____ = _____

Use your answers from above to answer each question.

When you add two **even** numbers, is the answer even or odd?

When you add two **odd** numbers, is the answer even or odd?

When you add an **even** number plus an **odd** number, is the answer even or odd?

_____

Show what you know! Without adding, write if the answer will be even or odd.

4 + 7 will be ___ODD___ .   5 + 9 will be _____ .

11 + 16 will be _____ .   14 + 17 will be _____ .

20 + 36 will be _____ .   13 + 28 will be _____ .

33 + 15 will be _____ .   34 + 48 will be _____ .

Challenge yourself! Try it with bigger numbers.

357 + 248 will be _____ .

413 + 129 will be _____ .

672 + 190 will be _____ .

Let's Learn!

You can use place value blocks to show large numbers. To write the numbers, use a place value chart.

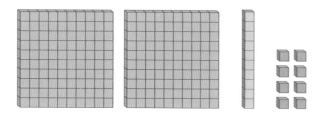

Hundreds	Tens	Ones
2	1	8

There are 2 hundreds, 1 ten, and 8 ones. This model shows 218.

Write the number for each model.

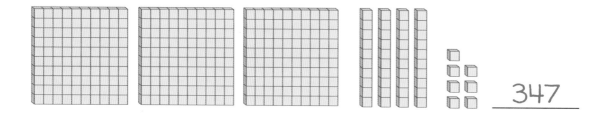

_347_

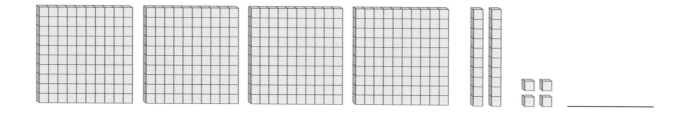

_____

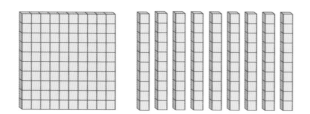

_____

Write the number for each model.

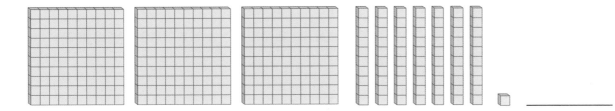

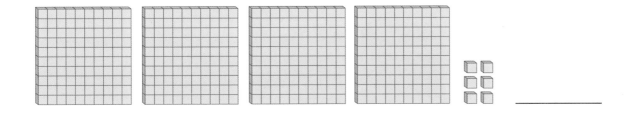

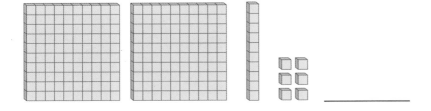

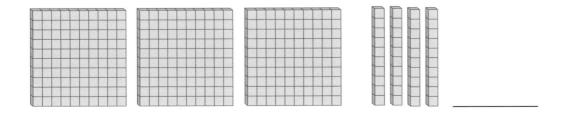

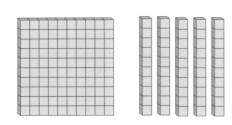

Let's Learn!

Each digit in a number has a place and a value. Let's find the place and value of each digit in 374!

Hundreds	Tens	Ones
3	7	4

Since 3 is in the **hundreds** place, it has a value of **300**.

Since 7 is in the **tens** place, it has a value of **70**.

Since 4 is in the **ones** place, it has a value of **4**.

Write the place and value of the highlighted **digit.**

4 **5** 2 _____TENS_____ _____50_____

9 7 1 _____ _____

2 9 **3** _____ _____

2 3 4 _____ _____

7 **3** 9 _____ _____

5 4 **7** _____ _____

9 **1** 8 _____ _____

IXL.com
skill ID
45U

Let's Learn!

You can use place value to write a number in **expanded form**. Expanded form shows the value of each digit in a number. Try it with 649!

649 = 600 + 40 + 9

expanded form

Write each number in expanded form.

207 = 200 + 7

563 = ____________

820 = ____________

926 = ____________

438 = ____________

103 = ____________

446 = ____________

317 = ____________

671 = ____________

560 = ____________

IXL.com skill ID HUX

Write each number.

300 + 60 + 7 = __367__

400 + 90 + 1 = _____

800 + 20 + 3 = _____

600 + 10 + 4 = _____

700 + 60 + 2 = _____

200 + 90 + 5 = _____

400 + 5 = _____

800 + 70 = _____

900 + 10 + 6 = _____

700 + 60 + 8 = _____

500 + 20 = _____

300 + 9 = _____

Write each number.

three hundred fifty-six 356

seven hundred sixty ______

nine hundred thirty-nine ______

four hundred ninety-one ______

Write the word name for each number.

173 ONE HUNDRED SEVENTY-THREE

821 ______

904 ______

514 ______

180 ______

IXL.com skill ID VPQ

Skip counting is counting by a number other than 1. Try it yourself!
Fill in the blanks to skip count by 10.

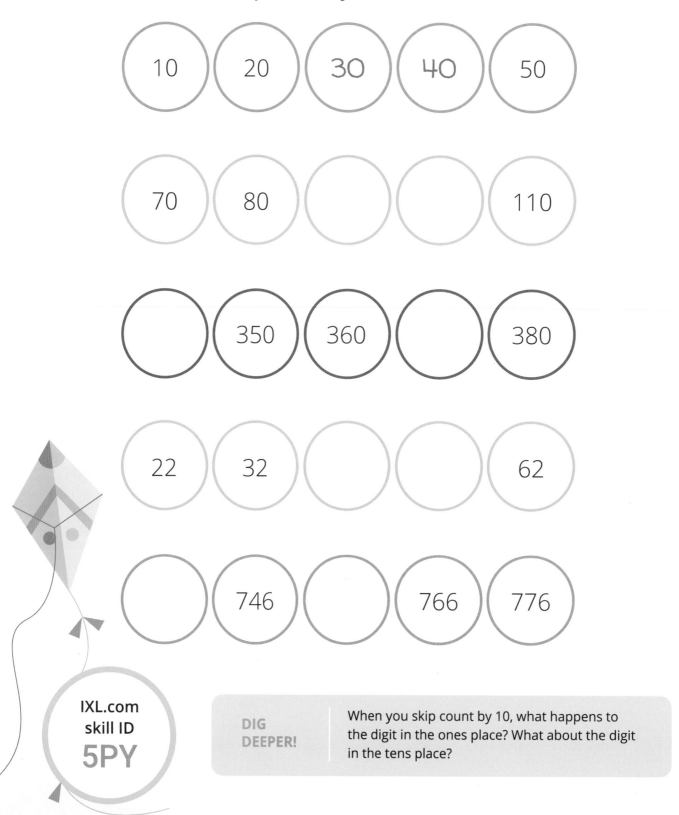

10 20 30 40 50

70 80 ⬤ ⬤ 110

⬤ 350 360 ⬤ 380

22 32 ⬤ ⬤ 62

⬤ 746 ⬤ 766 776

IXL.com
skill ID
5PY

DIG DEEPER! When you skip count by 10, what happens to the digit in the ones place? What about the digit in the tens place?

Keep it going! Fill in the blanks to skip count by 100.

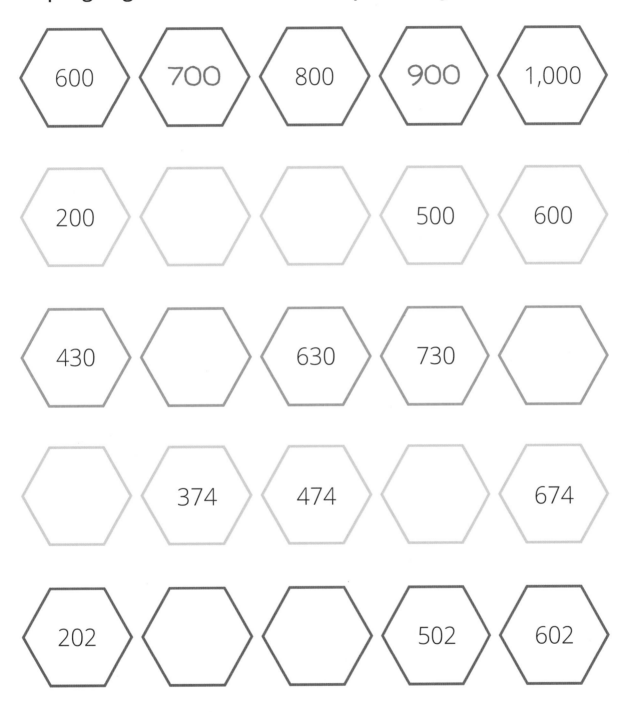

| 600 | 700 | 800 | 900 | 1,000 |

| 200 | | | 500 | 600 |

| 430 | | 630 | 730 | |

| | 374 | 474 | | 674 |

| 202 | | | 502 | 602 |

TAKE ANOTHER LOOK!

When you skip count by 100, what happens to the digits in each place? Which of the digits change?

Fill in the blanks to skip count by 5.

| 5 | 10 | 15 | 20 | 25 |

| 45 | 50 | | 60 | |

| 120 | 125 | | | 140 |

| 255 | | 265 | | 275 |

| 480 | 485 | | | 500 |

| | 695 | | 705 | 710 |

FIND THE PATTERN! | Look at the digits in the ones place in each problem. What pattern do you see?

Look at each skip-counting pattern. Write the missing numbers.

125 ___ 135 ___ 145 ___

611 ___ 631 ___ 651 ___

785 ___ ___ 800 ___ 810

___ 556 ___ 756 856 ___

IXL.com
skill ID
R5A

Let's Learn!

You can use place value to compare two numbers. Start with the digits in the greatest place value position. Look at the examples below to see how.

Hundreds	Tens	Ones
6	9	3
7	4	6

Hundreds	Tens	Ones
2	7	8
2	6	5

Since **6 hundreds** is less than **7 hundreds**, 693 is less than 746.

You can write this as 693 < 746.

Since **2 hundreds** is equal to **2 hundreds**, move to the tens place. Since **7 tens** is greater than **6 tens**, 278 is greater than 265.

You can write this as 278 > 265.

Compare the numbers. Write greater than, less than, or equal to on the line. Then fill in each circle with >, <, or =.

382 is <u>**GREATER THAN**</u> 294.

382 ⊗ 294

467 is _____ 521.

467 ◯ 521

872 is _____ 728.

872 ◯ 728

302 is _____ 302.

302 ◯ 302

Fill in each circle with >, <, or =.

419 **>** 194   824 ◯ 428

783 ◯ 837   365 ◯ 563

507 ◯ 507   915 ◯ 951

812 ◯ 879   322 ◯ 313

Challenge yourself! Write a digit that would make each statement true.

[3] 45 < 479   3 [ ] 7 > 329

401 < [ ] 01   583 < 5 [ ] 2

[ ] 85 = 685

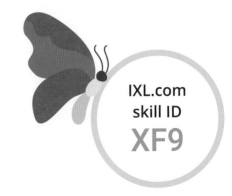

IXL.com
skill ID
XF9

Let's Learn!

You can use place value to add larger numbers! Add the **ones** first, the **tens** second, and the **hundreds** last.

$$
\begin{array}{r}
3\,1\,6 \\
+\,1\,5\,2 \\
\hline
8
\end{array}
\qquad
\begin{array}{r}
3\,1\,6 \\
+\,1\,5\,2 \\
\hline
6\,8
\end{array}
\qquad
\begin{array}{r}
3\,1\,6 \\
+\,1\,5\,2 \\
\hline
4\,6\,8
\end{array}
$$

So, 316 + 152 = 468!

Add.

$$
\begin{array}{r}
2\,4\,7 \\
+\,2\,5\,1 \\
\hline
4\,9\,8
\end{array}
\qquad
\begin{array}{r}
2\,3\,4 \\
+\,3\,6\,2 \\
\hline
\end{array}
\qquad
\begin{array}{r}
6\,2\,5 \\
+\,2\,0\,4 \\
\hline
\end{array}
$$

$$
\begin{array}{r}
4\,8\,5 \\
+\,1\,0\,2 \\
\hline
\end{array}
\qquad
\begin{array}{r}
2\,1\,6 \\
+\,4\,2\,3 \\
\hline
\end{array}
\qquad
\begin{array}{r}
3\,2\,1 \\
+\,3\,2\,0 \\
\hline
\end{array}
$$

$$
\begin{array}{r}
7\,4\,6 \\
+\,2\,4\,0 \\
\hline
\end{array}
\qquad
\begin{array}{r}
2\,2\,7 \\
+\,5\,5\,2 \\
\hline
\end{array}
\qquad
\begin{array}{r}
8\,3\,3 \\
+\,1\,6\,4 \\
\hline
\end{array}
$$

Let's Learn!

Sometimes you need to regroup when you add larger numbers. Look at the example to see how.

$$
\begin{array}{r}
\overset{1}{2}8\overset{\frown}{3} \\
+\ 1\ 2\ 9 \\
\hline
2
\end{array}
\qquad
\begin{array}{r}
\overset{1}{2}\overset{\frown}{8}\overset{1}{3} \\
+\ 1\ 2\ 9 \\
\hline
1\ 2
\end{array}
\qquad
\begin{array}{r}
\overset{\frown}{\overset{1}{2}}\,\overset{1}{8}\,3 \\
+\ 1\ 2\ 9 \\
\hline
4\ 1\ 2
\end{array}
$$

So, 283 + 129 = 412!

Add.

$$
\begin{array}{r}
4\overset{1}{2}7 \\
+\ 2\ 1\ 3 \\
\hline
6\ 4\ 0
\end{array}
\qquad
\begin{array}{r}
2\ 5\ 1 \\
+\ 1\ 7\ 3 \\
\hline
\end{array}
\qquad
\begin{array}{r}
5\ 0\ 9 \\
+\ 1\ 1\ 6 \\
\hline
\end{array}
$$

$$
\begin{array}{r}
3\ 2\ 4 \\
+\ 2\ 8\ 7 \\
\hline
\end{array}
\qquad
\begin{array}{r}
4\ 4\ 9 \\
+\ 2\ 4\ 8 \\
\hline
\end{array}
\qquad
\begin{array}{r}
2\ 5\ 5 \\
+\ 2\ 7\ 6 \\
\hline
\end{array}
$$

$$
\begin{array}{r}
5\ 3\ 4 \\
+\ 1\ 8\ 7 \\
\hline
\end{array}
\qquad
\begin{array}{r}
4\ 8\ 6 \\
+\ 4\ 8\ 6 \\
\hline
\end{array}
$$

IXL.com
skill ID
ETW

Add.

```
   170          251          355
 + 427        + 119        + 203
 _____       _____       _____


   241          375          263
 + 188        + 125        + 645
 _____       _____       _____


   448          593          285
 + 312        + 126        + 377
 _____       _____       _____


   634          149          474
 + 223        + 756        + 308
 _____       _____       _____
```

Add.

$$\begin{array}{r} 126 \\ +235 \\ \hline \end{array}$$

$$\begin{array}{r} 247 \\ +201 \\ \hline \end{array}$$

$$\begin{array}{r} 368 \\ +124 \\ \hline \end{array}$$

$$\begin{array}{r} 556 \\ +341 \\ \hline \end{array}$$

$$\begin{array}{r} 605 \\ +199 \\ \hline \end{array}$$

$$\begin{array}{r} 243 \\ +547 \\ \hline \end{array}$$

$$\begin{array}{r} 339 \\ +339 \\ \hline \end{array}$$

$$\begin{array}{r} 478 \\ +205 \\ \hline \end{array}$$

$$\begin{array}{r} 216 \\ +284 \\ \hline \end{array}$$

$$\begin{array}{r} 439 \\ +269 \\ \hline \end{array}$$

$$\begin{array}{r} 467 \\ +278 \\ \hline \end{array}$$

$$\begin{array}{r} 755 \\ +195 \\ \hline \end{array}$$

$$\begin{array}{r} 587 \\ +296 \\ \hline \end{array}$$

$$\begin{array}{r} 776 \\ +187 \\ \hline \end{array}$$

$$\begin{array}{r} 586 \\ +259 \\ \hline \end{array}$$

IXL.com
skill ID
R5W

Write the missing numbers. Each number in the pyramid is the sum of the two numbers below it.

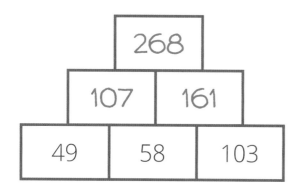

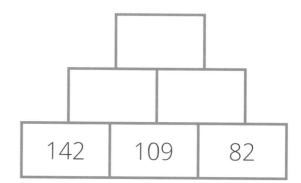

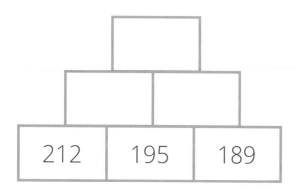

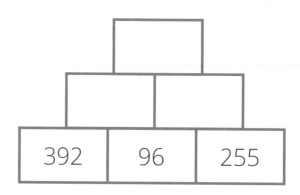

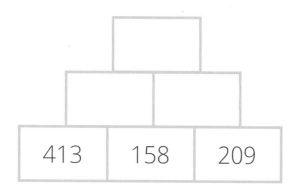

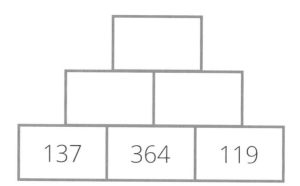

Answer each question.

Megan bought a new camera for her trip to the mountains. She took 124 pictures on her first day and 89 pictures on her second day. How many pictures did she take in all?

_____ pictures

The Allentown Zoo has two elephants, Coco and Henley. Coco eats 370 pounds of food each day. Henley eats 445 pounds of food each day. How many pounds of food do the elephants eat each day?

_____ pounds

Owen works at Perfect Bites Cupcake Shop. On Saturday, he made 275 cupcakes. On Sunday, he made 135 cupcakes. How many cupcakes did Owen make over the weekend?

_____ cupcakes

Mrs. Harrison is throwing a party. The food will cost $485. The party room will cost $429. How much will she pay for the food and the party room?

_____

IXL.com
skill ID
UV2

Let's Learn!

You can use place value to subtract larger numbers, too! Subtract the
ones first, the **tens** second, and the **hundreds** last.

$$
\begin{array}{r}
6\,3\,9 \\
-1\,3\,5 \\
\hline
4
\end{array}
\qquad
\begin{array}{r}
6\,3\,9 \\
-1\,3\,5 \\
\hline
0\,4
\end{array}
\qquad
\begin{array}{r}
6\,3\,9 \\
-1\,3\,5 \\
\hline
5\,0\,4
\end{array}
$$

So, 639 − 135 = 504!

Subtract.

$$
\begin{array}{r}
5\,6\,2 \\
-1\,5\,1 \\
\hline
4\,1\,1
\end{array}
\qquad
\begin{array}{r}
4\,5\,6 \\
-2\,1\,3 \\
\hline
\end{array}
\qquad
\begin{array}{r}
3\,2\,6 \\
-1\,2\,1 \\
\hline
\end{array}
$$

$$
\begin{array}{r}
6\,7\,4 \\
-5\,2\,3 \\
\hline
\end{array}
\qquad
\begin{array}{r}
9\,4\,7 \\
-4\,2\,5 \\
\hline
\end{array}
\qquad
\begin{array}{r}
8\,9\,8 \\
-7\,0\,4 \\
\hline
\end{array}
$$

$$
\begin{array}{r}
7\,0\,9 \\
-6\,0\,3 \\
\hline
\end{array}
\qquad
\begin{array}{r}
9\,9\,6 \\
-3\,8\,4 \\
\hline
\end{array}
\qquad
\begin{array}{r}
6\,9\,3 \\
-4\,7\,2 \\
\hline
\end{array}
$$

Subtract.

$$
\begin{array}{r} 439 \\ -229 \\ \hline \end{array}
\qquad
\begin{array}{r} 716 \\ -302 \\ \hline \end{array}
\qquad
\begin{array}{r} 583 \\ -261 \\ \hline \end{array}
$$

$$
\begin{array}{r} 984 \\ -582 \\ \hline \end{array}
\qquad
\begin{array}{r} 874 \\ -250 \\ \hline \end{array}
\qquad
\begin{array}{r} 338 \\ -215 \\ \hline \end{array}
$$

$$
\begin{array}{r} 649 \\ -627 \\ \hline \end{array}
\qquad
\begin{array}{r} 288 \\ -153 \\ \hline \end{array}
\qquad
\begin{array}{r} 499 \\ -387 \\ \hline \end{array}
$$

$$
\begin{array}{r} 982 \\ -261 \\ \hline \end{array}
\qquad
\begin{array}{r} 564 \\ -162 \\ \hline \end{array}
\qquad
\begin{array}{r} 887 \\ -456 \\ \hline \end{array}
$$

Let's Learn!

Sometimes you need to regroup when you subtract larger numbers. Start with the same steps as before.

$$
\begin{array}{r}
2\ \overset{\frown}{\ 16\ } \\
4\ \cancel{3}\ \cancel{6} \\
-\ 1\ 4\ 8 \\
\hline
8
\end{array}
$$

Subtract the **ones**. You can't do 6 − 8, so you need to borrow from the tens.

Cross out the 3 and write 2. Cross out the 6 and write 16. Now you can subtract.

$$
\begin{array}{r}
3\ \overset{\frown}{12}\ 16 \\
\cancel{4}\ \cancel{3}\ \cancel{6} \\
-\ 1\ 4\ 8 \\
\hline
8\ 8
\end{array}
$$

Keep going. Subtract the **tens**. You can't do 2 − 4, so you need to borrow from the hundreds.

Cross out the 4 and write 3. Change the 2 to a 12. Now you can subtract.

$$
\begin{array}{r}
\overset{\frown}{3}\ 12\ 16 \\
\cancel{4}\ \cancel{3}\ \cancel{6} \\
-\ 1\ 4\ 8 \\
\hline
2\ 8\ 8
\end{array}
$$

Finally, subtract the **hundreds**

So, 436 − 148 = 288!

Subtract.

$$
\begin{array}{r}
{\scriptstyle 6\ 14\ 14} \\
\cancel{754} \\
-159 \\
\hline
595
\end{array}
\qquad
\begin{array}{r}
592 \\
-273 \\
\hline
\end{array}
\qquad
\begin{array}{r}
693 \\
-286 \\
\hline
\end{array}
$$

$$
\begin{array}{r}
825 \\
-378 \\
\hline
\end{array}
\qquad
\begin{array}{r}
362 \\
-123 \\
\hline
\end{array}
\qquad
\begin{array}{r}
778 \\
-189 \\
\hline
\end{array}
$$

$$
\begin{array}{r}
714 \\
-624 \\
\hline
\end{array}
\qquad
\begin{array}{r}
831 \\
-469 \\
\hline
\end{array}
\qquad
\begin{array}{r}
513 \\
-279 \\
\hline
\end{array}
$$

Subtract. Follow the example.

$$
\begin{array}{r}
{\scriptstyle 59\ 15} \\
\cancel{605} \\
-379 \\
\hline
226
\end{array}
\qquad
\begin{array}{r}
803 \\
-546 \\
\hline
\end{array}
\qquad
\begin{array}{r}
602 \\
-254 \\
\hline
\end{array}
$$

$$
\begin{array}{r}
906 \\
-138 \\
\hline
\end{array}
\qquad
\begin{array}{r}
400 \\
-114 \\
\hline
\end{array}
$$

IXL.com
skill ID
ZVR

Subtract.

$$
\begin{array}{r}
895 \\
-106 \\
\hline
\end{array}
\qquad
\begin{array}{r}
653 \\
-277 \\
\hline
\end{array}
\qquad
\begin{array}{r}
924 \\
-659 \\
\hline
\end{array}
$$

$$
\begin{array}{r}
568 \\
-298 \\
\hline
\end{array}
\qquad
\begin{array}{r}
925 \\
-549 \\
\hline
\end{array}
\qquad
\begin{array}{r}
761 \\
-508 \\
\hline
\end{array}
$$

$$
\begin{array}{r}
713 \\
-407 \\
\hline
\end{array}
\qquad
\begin{array}{r}
922 \\
-608 \\
\hline
\end{array}
\qquad
\begin{array}{r}
500 \\
-238 \\
\hline
\end{array}
$$

$$
\begin{array}{r}
527 \\
-346 \\
\hline
\end{array}
\qquad
\begin{array}{r}
781 \\
-225 \\
\hline
\end{array}
\qquad
\begin{array}{r}
646 \\
-385 \\
\hline
\end{array}
$$

$$
\begin{array}{r}
800 \\
-543 \\
\hline
\end{array}
\qquad
\begin{array}{r}
479 \\
-189 \\
\hline
\end{array}
\qquad
\begin{array}{r}
514 \\
-298 \\
\hline
\end{array}
$$

IXL.com
skill ID
MDY

Subtract. Compare each pair of differences using >, <, or =.

$$380 - 278 \quad > \quad 521 - 453$$

$$
\begin{array}{r}
3 \, \overset{7}{\cancel{8}} \, \overset{10}{\cancel{0}} \\
-2 \, 7 \, 8 \\
\hline
1 \, 0 \, 2
\end{array}
\qquad
\begin{array}{r}
\overset{4}{\cancel{5}} \, \overset{11}{\cancel{2}} \, \overset{11}{\cancel{1}} \\
-4 \, 5 \, 3 \\
\hline
6 \, 8
\end{array}
$$

$$876 - 391 \quad \bigcirc \quad 724 - 409$$

$$625 - 267 \quad \bigcirc \quad 844 - 482$$

$$788 - 399 \quad \bigcirc \quad 765 - 379$$

IXL.com
skill ID
LSU

Answer each question.

Kayla and Reagan went on different airplanes during their spring break. Kayla counted 530 seats on her airplane. Reagan counted 185 seats on her airplane. How many more seats did Kayla's airplane have than Reagan's airplane?

_____ seats

Jimmy bought a laptop for $789. If Jimmy had $900 before he bought the laptop, how much money does he have now?

_____

Katie is on a road trip with her family. They are driving 835 miles to visit Katie's aunt. So far, they have driven 684 miles. How much farther do they need to drive?

_____ miles

Seth is building a model ship. The ship has 350 pieces. Seth has put 274 pieces together. How many more pieces does Seth need to add to finish the ship?

_____ pieces

Time to review! Add or subtract.

405 +391	564 −323	348 −256
683 +229	478 +513	573 −264
744 −356	253 −179	465 +275
608 +297	621 −345	346 +247
379 +338	904 −586	750 −476
686 +135	592 +348	911 −598

Add or subtract.

$$
\begin{array}{r}
784 \\
-297 \\
\hline
\end{array}
\qquad
\begin{array}{r}
346 \\
+355 \\
\hline
\end{array}
\qquad
\begin{array}{r}
631 \\
-428 \\
\hline
\end{array}
$$

$$
\begin{array}{r}
290 \\
+148 \\
\hline
\end{array}
\qquad
\begin{array}{r}
573 \\
+387 \\
\hline
\end{array}
\qquad
\begin{array}{r}
402 \\
-151 \\
\hline
\end{array}
$$

$$
\begin{array}{r}
632 \\
+274 \\
\hline
\end{array}
\qquad
\begin{array}{r}
511 \\
-343 \\
\hline
\end{array}
\qquad
\begin{array}{r}
329 \\
+489 \\
\hline
\end{array}
$$

$$
\begin{array}{r}
903 \\
-526 \\
\hline
\end{array}
\qquad
\begin{array}{r}
434 \\
-378 \\
\hline
\end{array}
\qquad
\begin{array}{r}
175 \\
+335 \\
\hline
\end{array}
$$

$$
\begin{array}{r}
318 \\
-276 \\
\hline
\end{array}
\qquad
\begin{array}{r}
269 \\
+463 \\
\hline
\end{array}
\qquad
\begin{array}{r}
548 \\
-268 \\
\hline
\end{array}
$$

Add or subtract to complete the puzzle.

ACROSS

2.
```
  786
- 139
```

4.
```
  256
+ 478
```

5.
```
  748
+ 167
```

7.
```
  255
+ 245
```

DOWN

1.
```
  931
- 424
```

2.
```
  996
- 347
```

3.
```
  391
+ 364
```

6.
```
  713
- 583
```

Follow the path from start to finish!

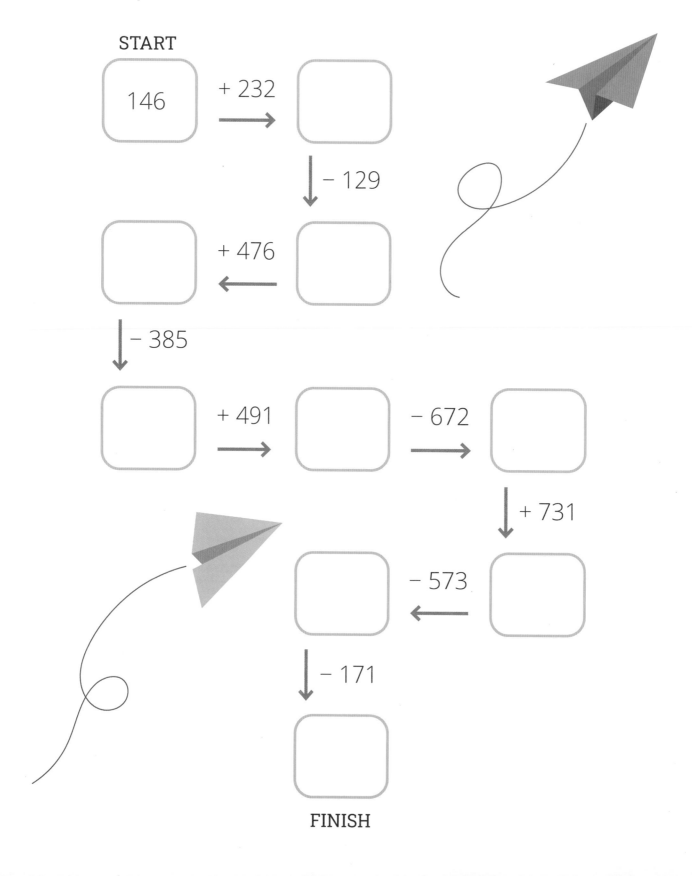

START

146 + 232 → ⬜

⬜ − 129 ↓

⬜ ← + 476 ⬜

− 385 ↓

⬜ + 491 → ⬜ − 672 → ⬜

+ 731 ↓

⬜ − 573 ← ⬜

− 171 ↓

⬜

FINISH

Answer each question.

Pedro went to a football game and a soccer game last week. There were 458 people at the football game. There were 243 people at the soccer game. How many more people were at the football game than the soccer game?

_____ people

Rusty works at a pretzel stand. Before he opens the stand, he makes 130 pretzels with salt and 110 pretzels without salt. How many pretzels does Rusty make?

_____ pretzels

Mallory's summer camp has a field day today. There are 236 campers playing games on the grass. There are 187 campers eating lunch in the food hall. How many campers is that in all?

_____ campers

Ben bought 565 stones to make a path. He used only 492 of the stones. How many stones does he have left over?

_____ stones

IXL.com
skill ID
XSH

Use a ruler to measure the length of each object in inches.

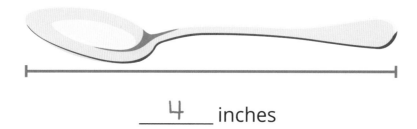

__4__ inches

_____ inches

_____ inches

_____ inches

IXL.com
skill ID
88A

For more practice, visit IXL.com or the IXL mobile app and enter this code in the search bar.

Keep going! Try it with centimeters.

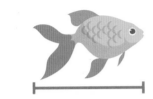

___3___ centimeters

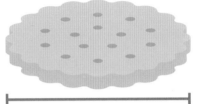

_____ centimeters

_____ centimeters

_____ centimeters

Let's Learn!

Some lengths are between two inch markers. You can measure to the nearest inch by choosing the closest number.

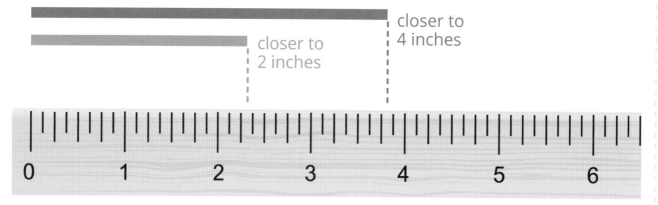

The first line is about 4 inches long. The second line is about 2 inches long.

Measure the length of each object to the nearest inch.

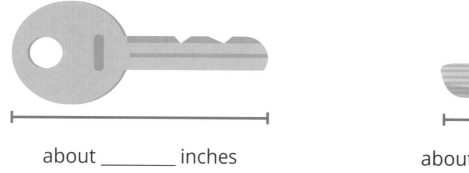

about _____ inches

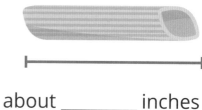

about _____ inches

about _____ inches

Measure the length of each object to the nearest centimeter.

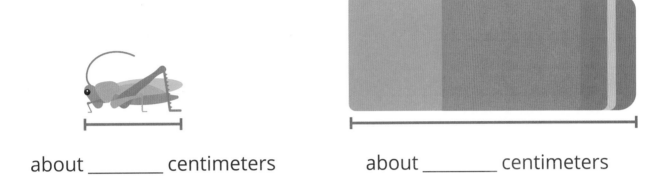

about _____ centimeters

about _____ centimeters

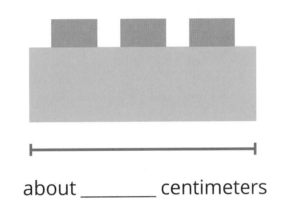

about _____ centimeters

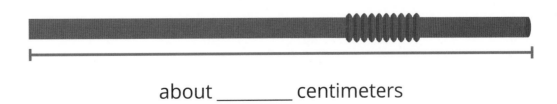

about _____ centimeters

Let's Learn!

You can use inches, feet, and yards to measure length.

A quarter is about 1 **inch** long.

A ruler is about 1 **foot** long.

A baseball bat is about 1 **yard** long.

You can think about these objects to **estimate** the length of other objects. When you estimate, you are making a close guess.

Fill in the blank with inches, feet, or yards to make an estimate.

A doorway is about 8 ____FEET____ tall.

A bookmark is about 8 _____ long.

A car is about 5 _____ long.

A bed is about 7 _____ long.

A cup is about 4 _____ tall.

Circle the better estimate.

Length of a bike

2 feet   (6 feet)

Height of an apple

4 inches   10 inches

Length of a table

10 inches   8 feet

Length of a school bus

5 feet   15 yards

Length of a hamster

3 inches   3 feet

Length of an ear of corn

8 inches   18 inches

Length of a fork

7 inches   2 feet

Length of a cow

2 yards   9 yards

Let's Learn!

You can also measure objects using centimeters and meters. You can use the examples below to help you estimate other lengths.

The width of your pointer finger is about 1 **centimeter**.

The height of a door handle is about 1 **meter**.

Fill in the blank with centimeters or meters to make an estimate.

A pen is about 12 __CENTIMETERS__ long.

A couch is about 3 _____ long.

A water bottle is about 20 _____ tall.

The stick on a mop is about 2 _____ long.

A minivan is about 5 _____ long.

A soup can is about 10 _____ tall.

IXL.com
skill ID
SKH

Circle the better estimate.

Length of a library card

2 centimeters   （8 centimeters）

Length of a house

2 meters   20 meters

Length of a glue stick

7 centimeters   7 meters

Length of a dollar bill

5 centimeters   16 centimeters

Length of a popsicle stick

3 centimeters   10 centimeters

Height of a cereal box

5 centimeters   30 centimeters

Length of a boat

14 centimeters   14 meters

Length of a truck

3 meters   12 meters

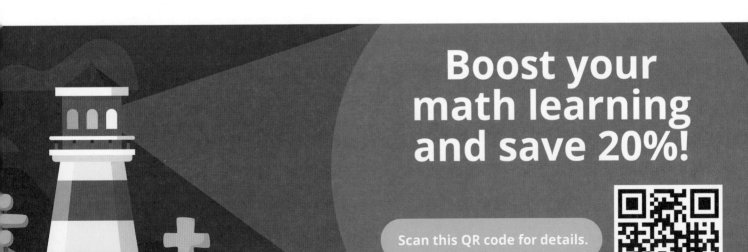

Estimate the height of each book in inches. Then use a ruler to measure each height. How close was your estimate?

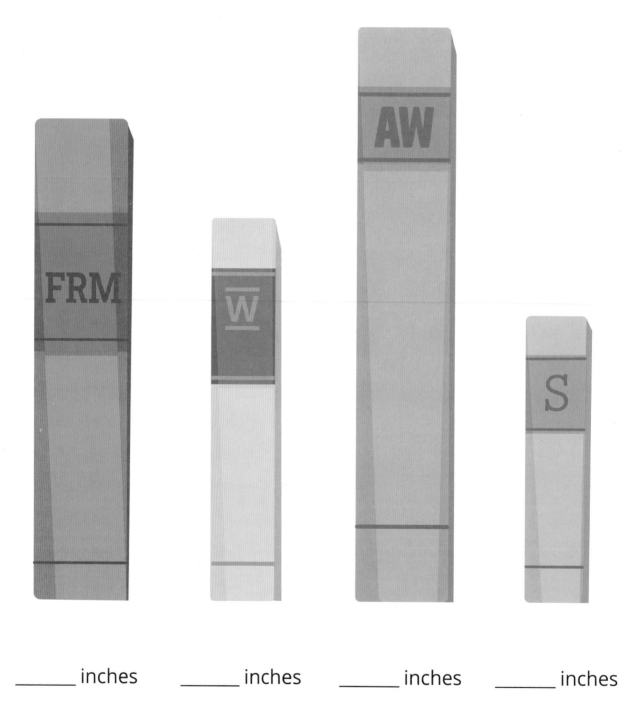

_____ inches _____ inches _____ inches _____ inches

Estimate the length of each bug in centimeters. Then use a ruler to measure each length. How close was your estimate?

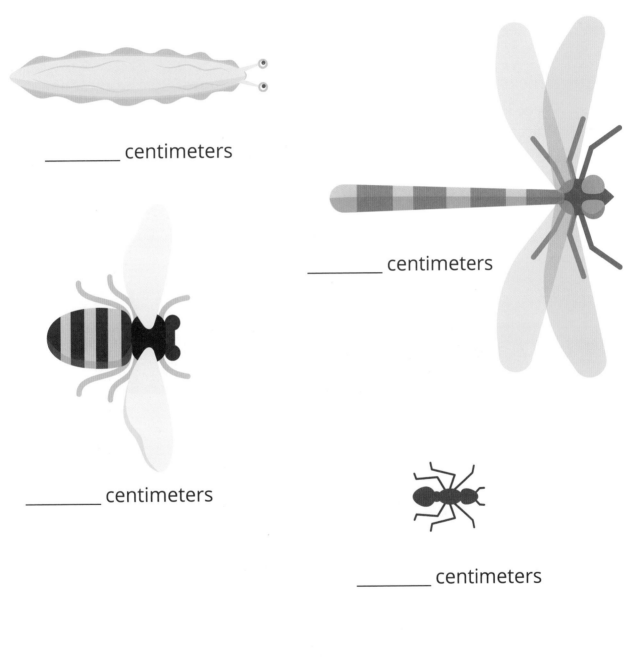

_____ centimeters

_____ centimeters

_____ centimeters

_____ centimeters

_____ centimeters

Let's Learn!

You can write measurements in different ways. Look at the examples below to see how.

This table is **1 yard** long. There are 3 feet in a yard. So, the table is also **3 feet** long.

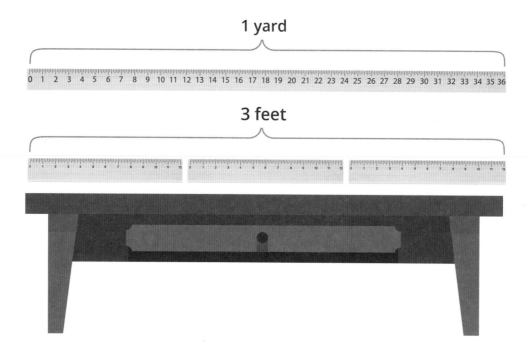

This notebook is **1 foot** long. There are 12 inches in a foot. So, the notebook is also **12 inches** long.

Fill in the blanks with inches, feet, or yards to make an estimate.

Height of a chair

about 48 __INCHES__   about 4 ____FEET____

Length of a horse

about 3 _____   about 9 _____

Height of a stop sign

about 5 _____   about 60 _____

Length of a fire truck

about 36 _____   about 12 _____

Height of a goose

about 1 _____   about 3 _____

Let's Learn!

You can write measurements in centimeters and meters, too.

For example, this guitar is **1 meter** long. There are 100 centimeters in a meter. So, the guitar is also **100 centimeters** long.

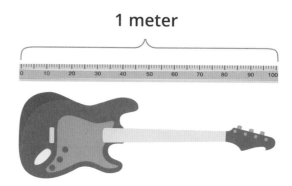

1 meter

Fill in the blanks with centimeters or meters to make an estimate.

Length of a park bench

about 2 _____METERS_____   about 200 CENTIMETERS

Height of a flagpole

about 5 _____   about 500 _____

Length of golf club

about 100 _____   about 1 _____

Height of an elephant

about 400 _____   about 4 _____

You can find the distance around a shape by adding all of the side lengths. Try it for the rectangle below!

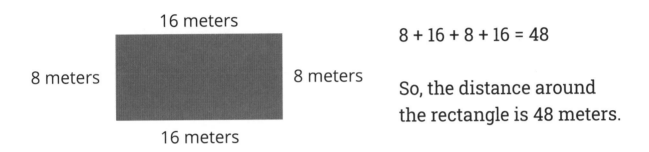

16 meters

8 meters   8 meters

16 meters

8 + 16 + 8 + 16 = 48

So, the distance around the rectangle is 48 meters.

Find the distance around each rectangle.

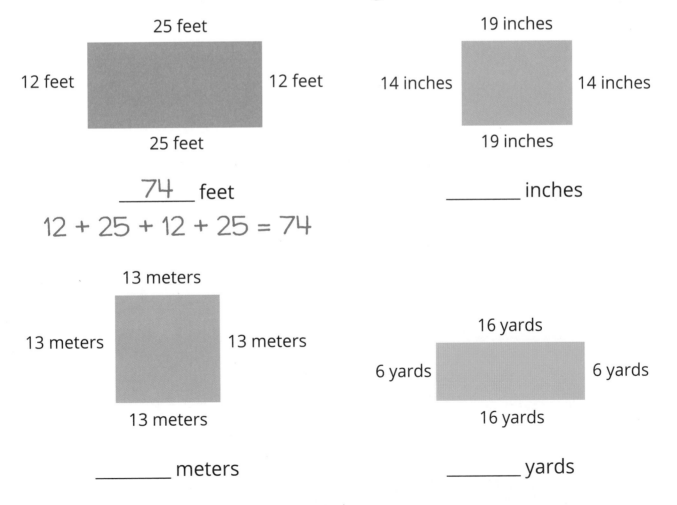

25 feet

12 feet   12 feet

25 feet

___74___ feet

12 + 25 + 12 + 25 = 74

19 inches

14 inches   14 inches

19 inches

_____ inches

13 meters

13 meters   13 meters

13 meters

_____ meters

16 yards

6 yards   6 yards

16 yards

_____ yards

Find the distance around each shape.

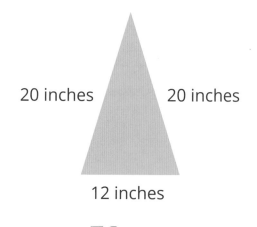

20 inches   20 inches

12 inches

_____52_____ inches

20 + 20 + 12 = 52

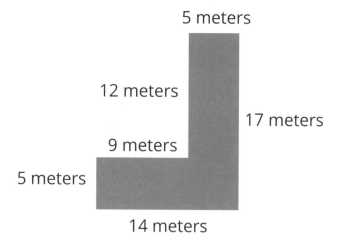

6 yards   10 yards

8 yards

_____ yards

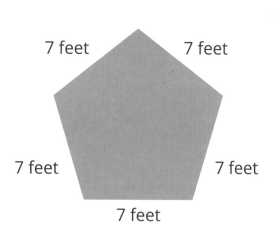

7 feet   7 feet

7 feet   7 feet

7 feet

_____ feet

5 meters

12 meters

17 meters

9 meters

5 meters

14 meters

_____ meters

IXL.com
skill ID
NP9

Answer each question.

Jasmin measured her TV and her laptop. Her TV is 54 inches wide. Her laptop is 13 inches wide. How much wider is Jasmin's TV than her laptop?

_____ inches

Jacob's football team had a game today. Before halftime, Jacob ran the ball 28 yards. After halftime, he ran the ball 30 yards. How many yards did Jacob run the ball in all?

_____ yards

Micah is at Windjammer Park. He walks 53 meters from the parking lot to the Ferris wheel. He then walks another 27 meters to the Spin Master ride. How far has he walked?

_____ meters

Haley's pumpkin pie needs to bake for 40 minutes. It has been in the oven for 12 minutes so far. How many more minutes does it need in the oven?

_____ minutes

Answer each question.

Juan built a robot that is 42 centimeters tall. His brother Diego built a robot that is 36 centimeters tall. How much taller is Juan's robot than Diego's?

_____ centimeters

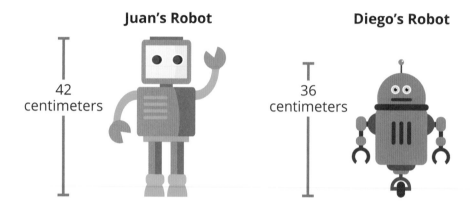

Juan's Robot

42 centimeters

Diego's Robot

36 centimeters

The boardwalk at Wilson Beach is 18 meters long. If Sophia walked to the end and back, how far did she walk?

_____ meters

Antonio is 122 centimeters tall. His sister Emily is 27 centimeters shorter than he is. How tall is Emily?

_____ centimeters

Marisol ran as fast as she could for 79 yards. She then walked 23 yards before she stopped. How far did Marisol go?

_____ yards

IXL.com
skill ID
KJ5

Solve the logic puzzle.

Five friends measured their heights. Use the clues to match the friends to their heights.

Tony is 3 inches taller than Gia.

Eli is 11 inches shorter than Gia.

Sean is 14 inches shorter than Stephanie.

Height	Tony	Gia	Stephanie	Eli	Sean
42 inches					
48 inches					
53 inches					
56 inches					
62 inches					

Let's Learn!

Below you can see each type of coin and its value.

Penny	Nickel	Dime	Quarter

1 cent	5 cents	10 cents	25 cents
1¢	5¢	10¢	25¢

Count on to find the value of the coins.

__10__ ¢   __20__ ¢   __21__ ¢

Total value: __21__ ¢

_____ ¢   _____ ¢   _____ ¢

Total value: _____ ¢

_____ ¢   _____ ¢   _____ ¢

Total value: _____ ¢

Count on to find the value of the coins.

Total value: __50__ ¢

__25__ ¢   __35__ ¢   __45__ ¢   __50__ ¢

Total value: _____ ¢

_____ ¢   _____ ¢   _____ ¢   _____ ¢

Total value: _____ ¢

_____ ¢   _____ ¢   _____ ¢   _____ ¢

Total value: _____ ¢

_____ ¢   _____ ¢   _____ ¢   _____ ¢

Total value: _____ ¢

_____ ¢   _____ ¢   _____ ¢   _____ ¢

IXL.com
skill ID
DGK

Find the value of the coins.

_36_ ¢

_____ ¢

_____ ¢

_____ ¢

THINK ABOUT IT! | When you count coins, is it easier to start with quarters or pennies?

IXL.com
skill ID
MGA

Find the value of the coins. Then circle the group with the largest value on the page.

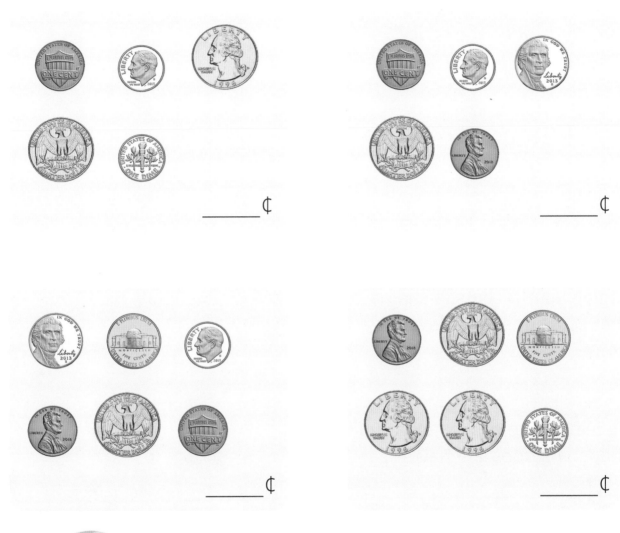

_____ ¢

_____ ¢

_____ ¢

_____ ¢

CHALLENGE ZONE

Answer each question.

Susie has 2 coins. If she has 15 cents, what coins does she have?

<u>1 DIME, 1 NICKEL</u>

Troy has 3 of the same type of coin. He has 30 cents in all. What coins does he have?

_____

Maggie has 11 cents. If she has 3 coins, what coins does she have?

_____

Annie has 3 coins. If she has 60 cents, what coins does she have?

_____

Dustin has 4 coins. What is the smallest amount of money he could have?

_____

Below you can see different types of bills and their values.

1-dollar bill

$1

5-dollar bill

$5

10-dollar bill

$10

20-dollar bill

$20

Count on to find the value of the bills.

$ __20__ $ __30__ $ __35__

Total value:

$ ___35___

$ _____ $ _____ $ _____

Total value:

$ _____

Count on to find the value of the bills.

$ __20__ $ __30__ $ __35__ $ __40__

Total value: $ __40__

$ _____ $ _____ $ _____ $ _____

Total value: $ _____

$ _____ $ _____ $ _____ $ _____

Total value: $ _____

$ _____ $ _____ $ _____ $ _____

Total value: $ _____

Find the value of the bills.

$ ___31___

$ _____

$ _____

$ _____

$ _____

$ _____

Find the value of the bills. Then circle the group with the largest value on the page.

$ _____

$ _____

$ _____

$ _____

Sandy, Jerry, and Max each walk dogs to earn money. The money that each person made last week is below. Use the clues to match each person to the money he or she made.

Clues

- Sandy made the most money.
- Jerry made less money than Max.

$ _____

Person:

_____

$ _____

Person:

_____

$ _____

Person:

_____

Let's Learn!

You can write dollars and cents using a decimal point. The number of dollars comes before the decimal point. The number of cents comes after the decimal point. Remember to use a dollar sign.

10 dollars and 31 cents
$10.31

Write the total value of the coins and bills.

$5.07

_____

_____

_____

IXL.com
skill ID
3R8

Show the items in the tally chart.

Ball	Tally
🏈	ⵑⵑⵑⵑ⧸
🏀	
🎾	

Animal	Tally
🦆	
🦆	
🐸	

Shell	Tally
🐚	
🐚	
🐚	

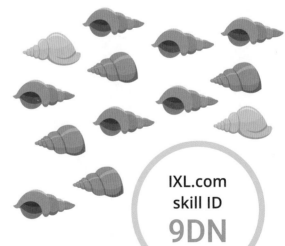

IXL.com
skill ID
9DN

Jillian asked some friends their favorite food. She showed their answers in a tally chart.

Favorite food	Number of friends
 Pizza	‖‖‖
Mac and cheese	‖‖‖ ‖
Tacos	‖

Use the tally chart to complete the bar graph.

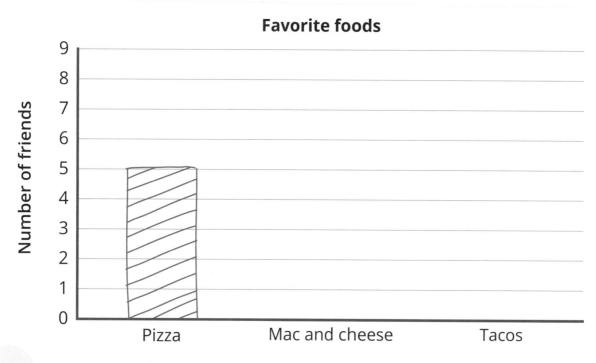

Favorite foods

Malcolm asked his friends their favorite zoo animal. He showed their answers in a tally chart.

Favorite zoo animal	Number of friends
Zebra	卌 l
Elephant	llll
Lion	lll
Monkey	卌 ll

Use the tally chart to complete the bar graph.

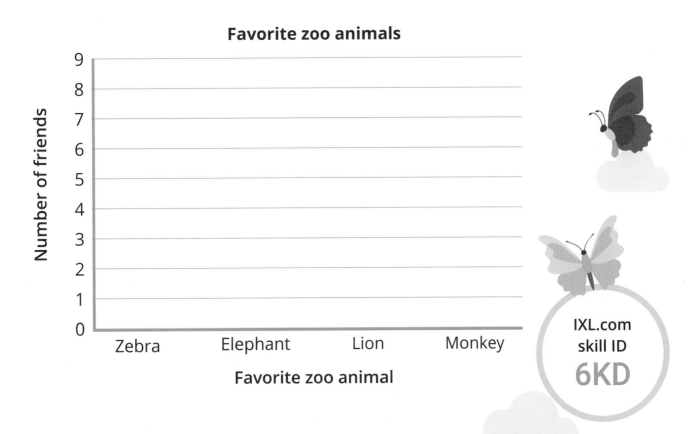

Favorite zoo animals

Number of friends

9
8
7
6
5
4
3
2
1
0

Zebra   Elephant   Lion   Monkey

Favorite zoo animal

Ross asked some friends what they did last weekend. He showed their answers on a bar graph.

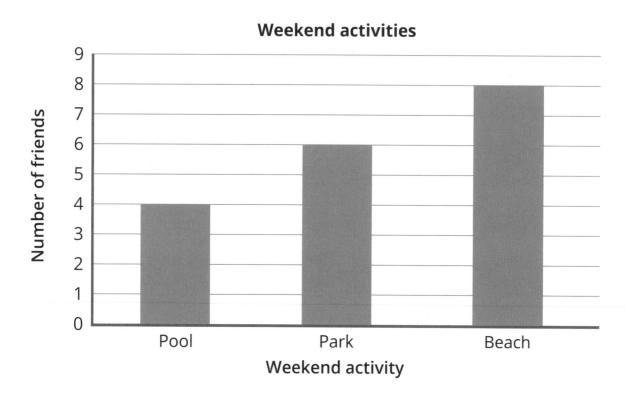

Answer each question.

How many people went to a pool?   _____ people

Where did exactly 6 people go?   _____

Where did the most people go?   _____

How many more people went to the beach than to a pool?

_____ people

Allen works at a bakery. He made a bar graph of the cake flavors that people ordered in the last week.

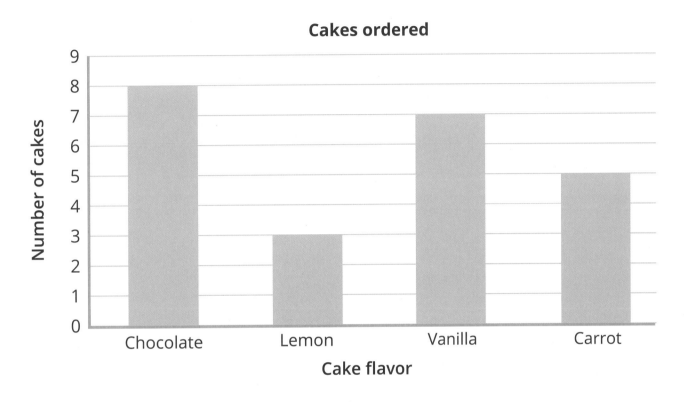

Answer each question.

How many vanilla cakes did people order?   _____ cakes

Which cake flavor was ordered the least?   _____

How many more chocolate cakes did people order than carrot cakes?   _____ cakes

How many cakes did people order in all?

_____ cakes

IXL.com
skill ID
8CH

Greg has the coins below. He showed his coins on a tally chart.

Type of coin	Number of coins
Penny	‖‖‖ ‖‖
Nickel	‖‖
Dime	‖‖‖
Quarter	‖

Use the tally chart to complete the bar graph.

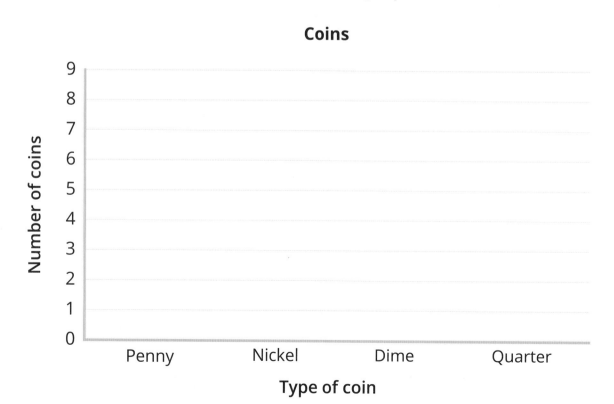

Coins

Number of coins

Penny   Nickel   Dime   Quarter

Type of coin

Answer each question about Greg's coins.

How much money does Greg have in nickels? _____ ¢

How much money does Greg have in dimes? _____ ¢

Does Greg have more money in pennies or nickels? _____

Does Greg have more money in dimes or quarters? _____

How much more money does Greg have in quarters than nickels? _____ ¢

How much more money does Greg have in dimes than pennies? _____ ¢

How much money does Greg have in all? _____ ¢

The students at Nina's school are selling boxes of cookies. Each grade wants to sell the most cookies. The tally chart shows how many boxes were sold on the first day.

Grade	Number of boxes sold
1st grade	|||||
2nd grade	||||| |||
3rd grade	|||

Use the tally chart to complete the pictograph.

Boxes of cookies sold	
1st grade	▭ ▭ ▭ ▭ ▭
2nd grade	
3rd grade	

Each ▭ = 1 box sold

Jonah and his friends are at the park. The tally chart shows the activity each friend chose.

Activity	Number of friends
Four square	ЖІІ
Tag	ЖЖ І
Swings	ІІІІ
Playground	ІІ

Use the tally chart to complete the pictograph.

Park activities	
Four square	
Tag	
Swings	
Playground	

Each 👤 = 1 friend

Jane gathered paper, glass, and plastic items to recycle. She showed the items she had on a pictograph.

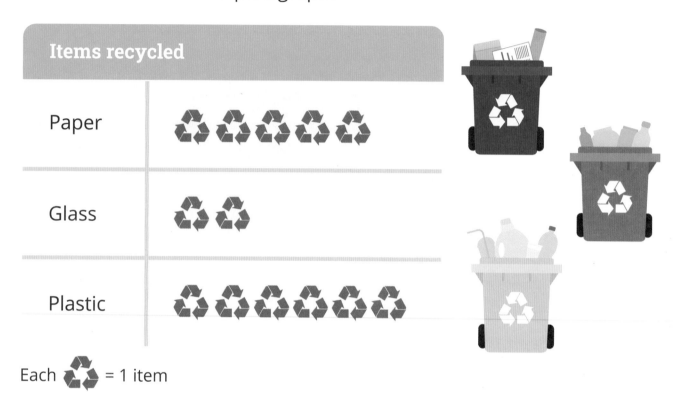

Items recycled

Paper	♻♻♻♻♻
Glass	♻♻
Plastic	♻♻♻♻♻♻

Each ♻ = 1 item

Answer each question.

Which kind of item did Jane gather the most of? _____

How many glass items did Jane have? _____ glass items

How many more paper items than glass items did Jane have? _____ paper items

How many items did Jane gather in all?

_____ items

IXL.com
skill ID
QDT

Liam asked his friends to pick their favorite season. He showed their answers on a pictograph.

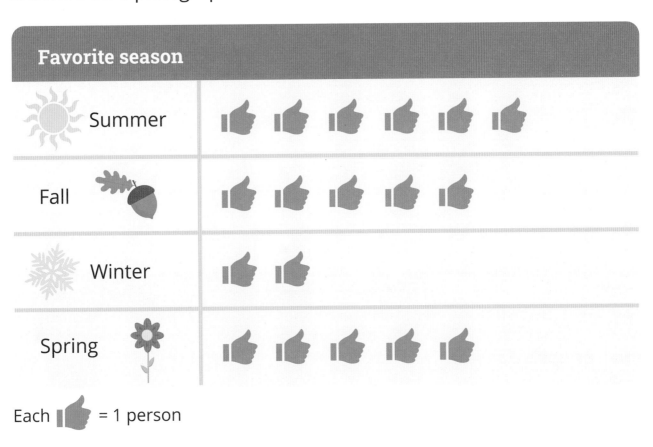

Each 👍 = 1 person

Answer each question.

How many people like summer the best? _____ people

Which two seasons have the same number of picks? _____

Which season did the fewest people pick? _____

How many people like spring or summer the best?

_____ people

IXL.com
skill ID
YL6

Amber asked her friends how many siblings they have. She showed their answers on a line plot.

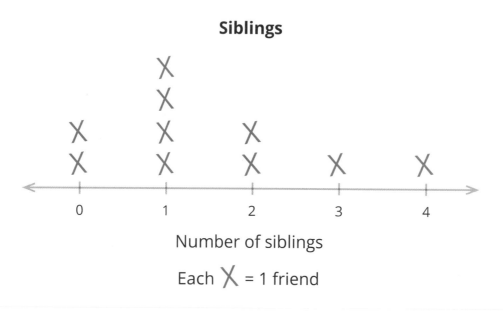

Siblings

Number of siblings

Each X = 1 friend

Answer each question.

How many friends have 0 siblings?   _____ friends

How many more friends have 1 sibling than 3 siblings?   _____ friends

How many friends have 1 or 2 siblings?   _____ friends

How many friends did Amber ask?   _____ friends

Dylan asked his friends how many pets they have. He showed their answers on a line plot.

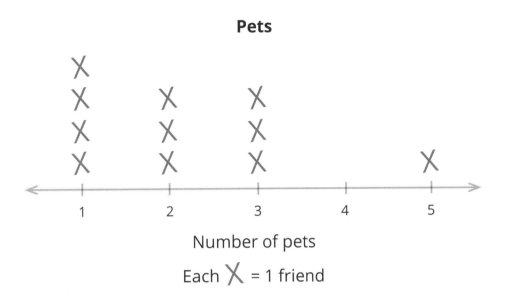

Answer each question.

Do more friends have 2 pets or 5 pets?   _____

How many friends have 1 pet?   _____ friends

How many friends have 3 or more pets?   _____ friends

How many more friends have 1 pet than 5 pets?   _____ friends

IXL.com
skill ID
HY6

Kelly wrote down the time it took her to get to school each day.

Time (in minutes)				
~~13~~	12	14	15	15
13	13	13	14	13

Use the table to complete the line plot.

Time to school

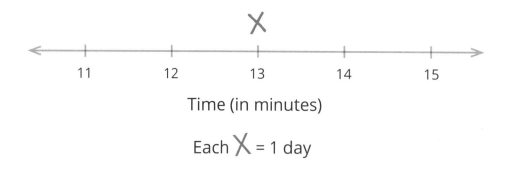

Time (in minutes)

Each ✗ = 1 day

Dave teaches a gardening class at Sunshine Shores Summer Camp. He wrote down the ages of the children in his class.

Ages (in years)						
7	6	6	7	8	9	10
6	7	5	6	7	10	7
8	7	7	9	5	6	8

Use the table to complete the line plot.

Ages of children in Dave's gardening class

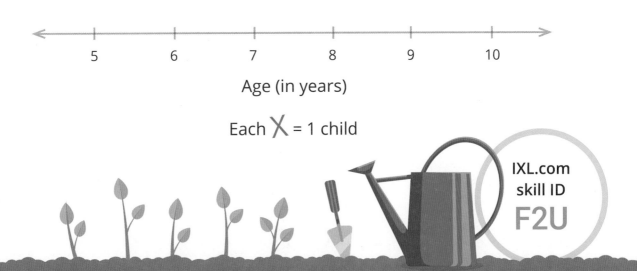

Age (in years)

Each ✗ = 1 child

Measure the length of each fishhook. Then record each length on the line plot.

3 INCHES

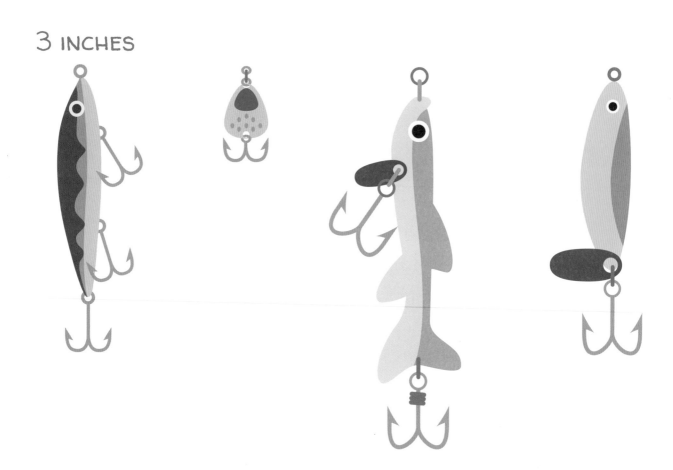

Lengths of fishhooks

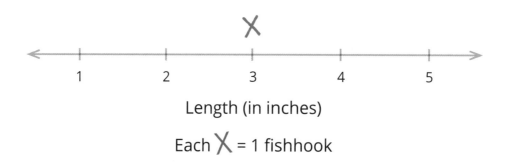

Length (in inches)

Each X = 1 fishhook

Measure the length of each feather. Then record each length on the line plot.

Lengths of feathers

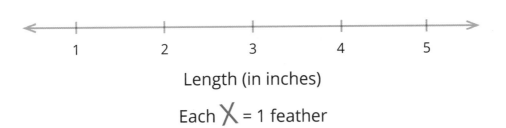

Length (in inches)

Each X = 1 feather

Exploration Zone

SORTING INFORMATION

You can show information in a **Venn diagram**. A Venn diagram is made up of circles that cross. Look at the example below.

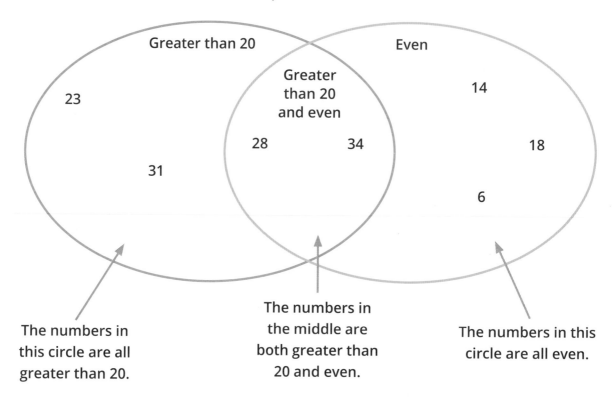

The numbers in this circle are all greater than 20.

The numbers in the middle are both greater than 20 and even.

The numbers in this circle are all even.

TRY IT YOURSELF!

Put each of the numbers into the Venn diagram above.

10   27   22

Keep it going! Complete each Venn diagram.

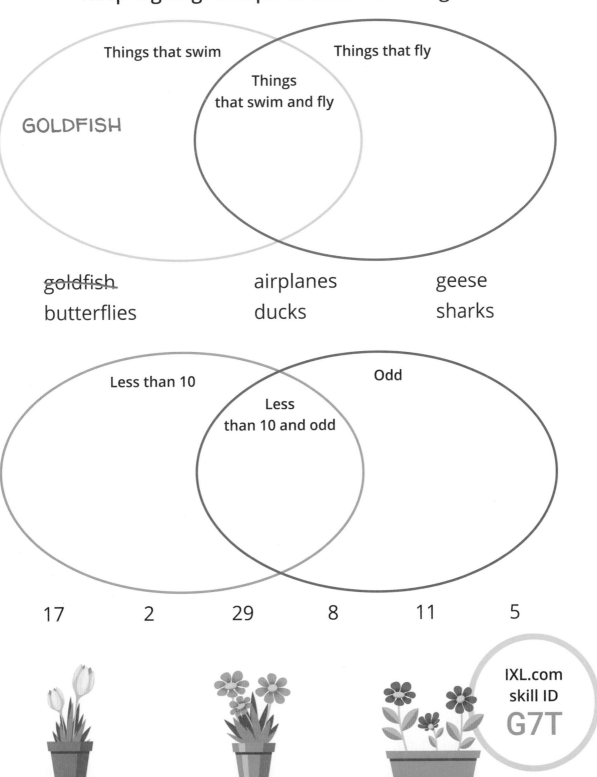

Things that swim

Things that fly

Things that swim and fly

GOLDFISH

~~goldfish~~   airplanes   geese
butterflies   ducks   sharks

Less than 10   Odd

Less than 10 and odd

17   2   29   8   11   5

Write the time shown on each clock.

_1:30_
_____

_____

_____

_____

_____

_____

Let's Learn!

On a clock, it takes 5 minutes for the minute hand to get from one number to the next. So, you can skip count by 5 to find the number of minutes that have passed.

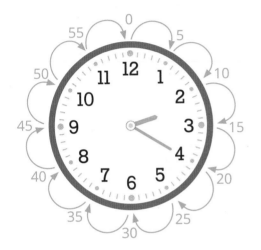

The **hour hand** is between 2 and 3. So, it is after 2:00 but before 3:00.

The **minute hand** points to 4. Skip count by 5 four times to find the number of minutes.

This clock shows the time is 2:20!

Write the time shown on each clock.

7:45

_____

_____

_____

IXL.com
skill ID
D9K

Draw a line between the matching times.

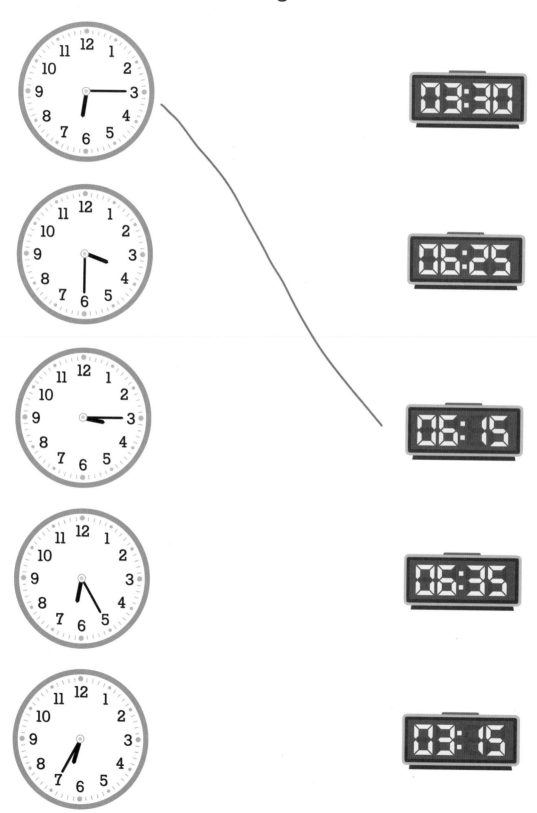

Draw hands on the clock to show the time.

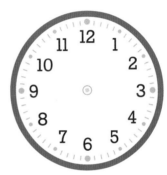 

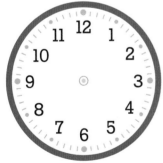 

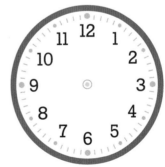 

Let's Learn!

You can say times in different ways. Look below to see different ways to say each time.

15 minutes to 7

quarter to 7

15 minutes after 7

quarter past 7

half past 7

Circle a way to say each time.

quarter past 3

quarter to 3

10 minutes after 2

quarter past 2

half past 11

half past 12

quarter past 6

half past 6

5 minutes to 4

5 minutes after 4

quarter past 1

quarter to 1

Answer each question.

Carmen gets to her painting class 10 minutes before 5:00. What time does she get there?

_____

 This clock shows when her painting class starts. Is Carmen early or late for class?

_____

Carmen begins cleaning up at 20 minutes after 6. What time does she start cleaning?

_____

Carmen leaves her class at half past 6. What time does Carmen leave?

_____

Carmen gets home at 6:45. What is another way to say this time?

_____

IXL.com
skill ID
5TA

Let's Learn!

You can use **a.m.** and **p.m.** to tell different parts of the day. Use a.m. to tell time in the morning. Use p.m. to tell time in the afternoon.

Jace wakes up at 7:00 a.m.   Jace goes to bed at 9:15 p.m.

Circle a.m. or p.m. for each activity.

Riding your bike before dinner   Brushing your teeth in the morning

a.m.   (p.m.)   a.m.   p.m.

Eating a morning snack   Going on an afternoon walk

a.m.   p.m.   a.m.   p.m.

Watching a movie after dinner   Getting dressed for school

a.m.   p.m.   a.m.   p.m.

Answer each question.

It's the weekend! Jeremy wakes up at 8:30. Is it a.m. or p.m.?

_____

If Jeremy looks at the clock when he wakes up, what will he see?

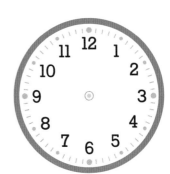

Jeremy has a soccer game at a quarter to 10. He checks the weather for the day. What will the weather be at the start of his game?

_____

After the game, Jeremy is going to a birthday party. The party starts at the time shown on the clock. What time does the party start?

_____

What is another way to say that time?

IXL.com
skill ID
EJV

_____

Complete the clocks with the start time and end time.

Eva goes to the park. She starts playing basketball at 3:15 p.m. She plays basketball for 30 minutes.

start time	end time

Rob is getting a haircut. He gets to the hairdresser at 11:10 a.m. His haircut takes 40 minutes.

start time	end time

Jackson is taking a flight up the West Coast. His airplane took off at 1:50 p.m. It will land 2 hours later.

start time	end time

Toby arrives at the pool at 12:30 p.m. He spends 3 hours there before heading home.

start time	end time

Complete the clocks with the start time and end time. Then tell how much time has passed.

Eric gets on a train at 9:05 a.m. He gets off the train at 9:40 a.m.

Melanie is in a dance show that starts at 4:30 p.m. The show ends at 7:30 p.m.

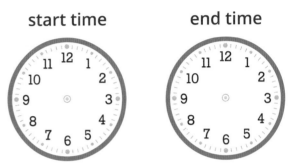

start time   end time

Time passed: __35__ minutes

Time passed: _____ hours

Ana's dad built a swing set in her backyard. He began at 8:30 a.m. He finished at 1:30 p.m.

Cody arrives at Frosty Cones Ice Cream Shop at 7:35 p.m. He leaves at 7:55 p.m.

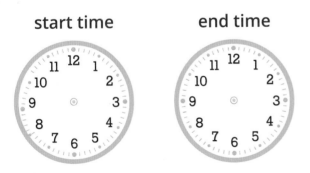

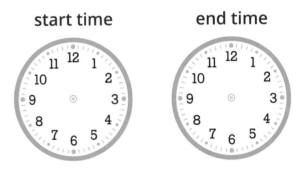

start time   end time

start time   end time

Time passed: _____ hours

Time passed: _____ minutes

Write the number of sides for each shape.

__3__

_____

_____

_____

_____

_____

_____

_____

_____

Let's Learn!

You can name shapes by the number of sides. Look below to see how.

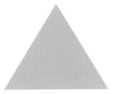

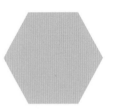

A **triangle**
has 3 sides.

A **quadrilateral**
has 4 sides.

A **pentagon**
has 5 sides.

A **hexagon**
has 6 sides.

Circle the name of each shape.

pentagon

hexagon

triangle

quadrilateral

triangle

pentagon

quadrilateral

pentagon

hexagon

pentagon

quadrilateral

hexagon

IXL.com
skill ID
2FK

Write the name of each shape.

_____PENTAGON_____

_____

_____

_____

_____

_____

_____

_____

_____

Draw each shape.

Draw a pentagon.

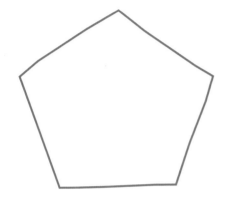

Draw a hexagon.

Draw a triangle.

Draw a quadrilateral.

Let's Learn!

Many shapes have **angles**. Angles are made when two sides in a shape meet.

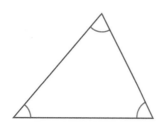

For example, a triangle has 3 angles.

Write the number of angles in each shape.

 _____5_____

 _____

 _____

 _____

 _____

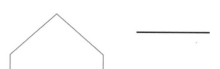 _____

Draw each shape. Then write the name of each shape.

Draw a shape with 4 angles.

__QUADRILATERAL__

Draw a shape with 3 angles.

_____

Draw a shape with 6 angles.

_____

Draw a shape with 5 angles.

_____

WAIT A MINUTE! Look at the number of sides and angles in each of your shapes. What do you notice? How many sides do you think a shape with 10 angles would have?

A **cube** is a three-dimensional shape with 6 **faces**. The faces are all squares.

A **face** is a flat side of a shape.

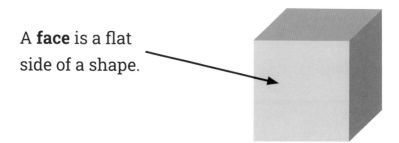

Circle the three cubes.

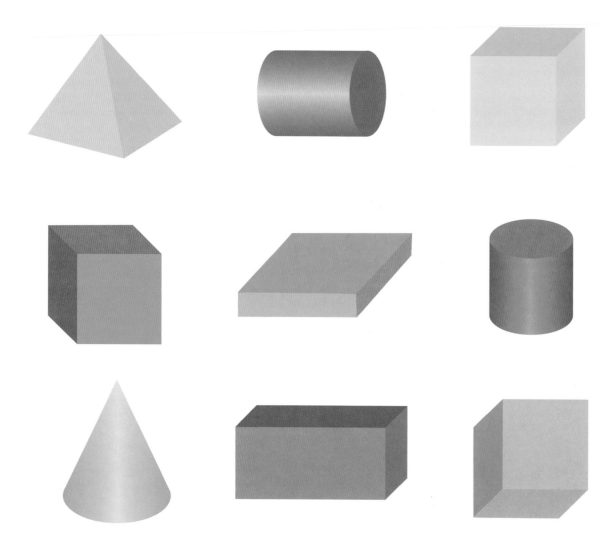

Circle the three cubes.

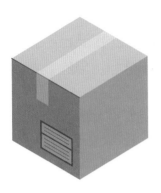

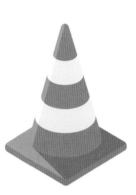

Let's Learn!

You can split shapes into pieces that are the same size. Each same-size piece is an **equal share**. Here are some examples of equal shares.

Circle each shape that is split into equal shares.

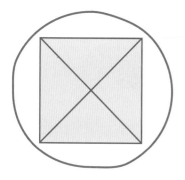

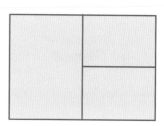

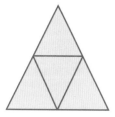
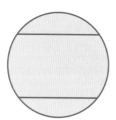
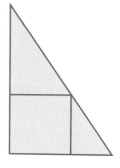

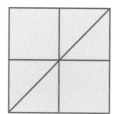

There are special names for different numbers of equal shares. Here are some of those names.

Halves
2 equal shares

Thirds
3 equal shares

Fourths
4 equal shares

Name the parts for each shape.

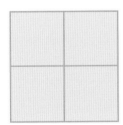

FOURTHS

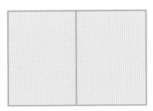

_____

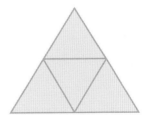

_____

_____

IXL.com
skill ID
24W

Split each shape into equal shares.

thirds

fourths

halves

halves

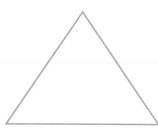

fourths

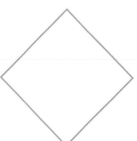

thirds

fourths

halves

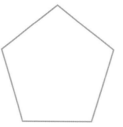

thirds

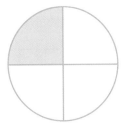

You can name one equal share of a shape.

For example, this circle shows fourths. Each piece of the circle is **one fourth**.

Write the name of each shaded piece.

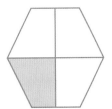

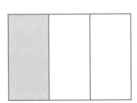

ONE HALF _____   _____   _____

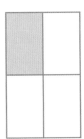

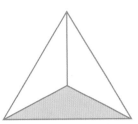

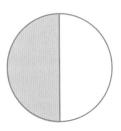

_____   _____   _____

Split and shade the shape to show the equal share.

one half

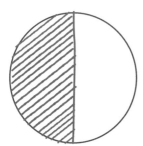

one third

one fourth

one third

one fourth

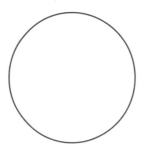

one half

one third

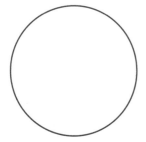

one half

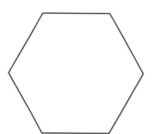

one fourth

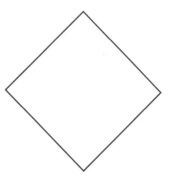

Split and shade the shape to show the equal share.

one fourth

one third

one half

one third

one half

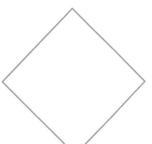

one fourth

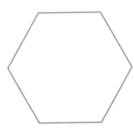

one half

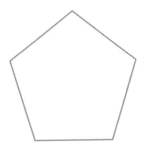

one fourth

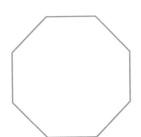

one half

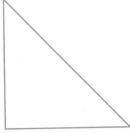

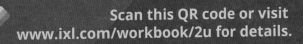

Let's Learn!

Here are some more special names for equal shares.

Sixths
6 equal shares

Eighths
8 equal shares

Name the parts for each shape.

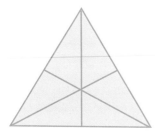

_____   _____   _____

Write the name of each shaded piece.

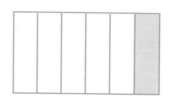

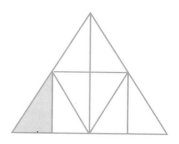

_____   _____   _____

Let's Learn!

You can name more than one equal share, too.

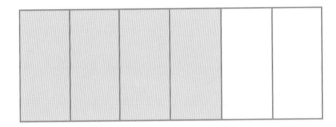

For example, this rectangle shows sixths. There are four shaded pieces. So, this rectangle shows **four sixths**.

Shade the shape to show the equal shares.

three fourths

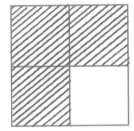

two halves

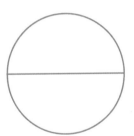

two thirds

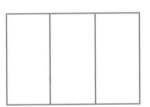

five eighths

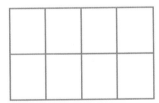

three sixths

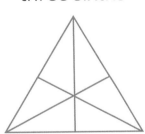

two fourths

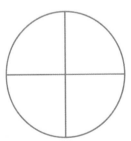

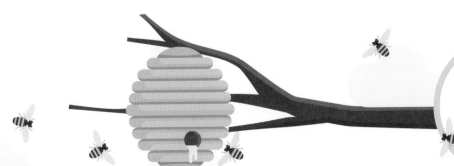

FRACTIONS

You can use a **fraction** to write a part of a whole. Fractions are made up of two numbers. The top number is the number of shaded pieces. The bottom number is the number of equal pieces in the whole.

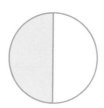

$$\frac{1}{2}$$ ← number of shaded pieces

← number of pieces in the whole

TRY IT YOURSELF!

Draw a line from the shape to the matching fraction.

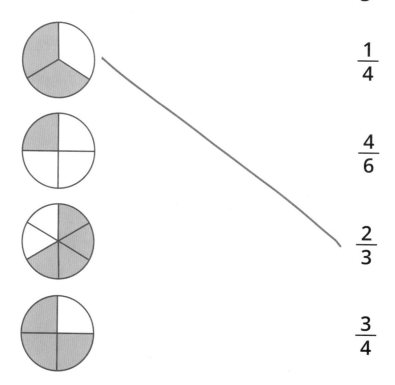

$$\frac{1}{4}$$

$$\frac{4}{6}$$

$$\frac{2}{3}$$

$$\frac{3}{4}$$

Keep going! Write the fraction for the shaded part of each shape.

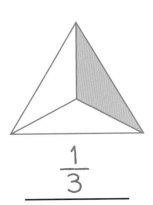

$$\frac{1}{3}$$
_____

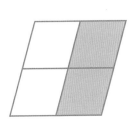

_____

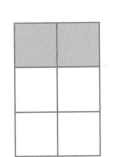

_____

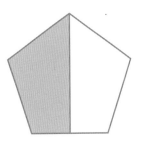

_____

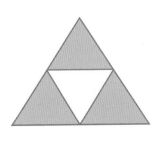

_____

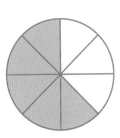

_____

IXL.com
skill ID
HVG

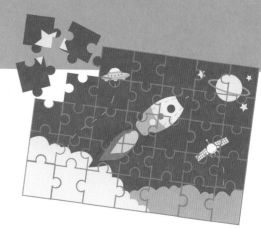

Alaina and Zach love jigsaw puzzles. They want to try a new puzzle together. Solve each problem.

Alaina and Zach go to the store to find a new puzzle. They pay for the puzzle with the bills below. How much money do they use to pay for the puzzle?

$ _____

Alaina and Zach get the change below. How much change do they get?

_____ ¢

The puzzle came in a box shaped like a cube. Circle the box.

Solve each problem.

Alaina and Zach start the puzzle at 1:15 p.m. They finish the puzzle at 1:40 p.m. Draw those times on the clocks. How much time do Alaina and Zach spend putting the puzzle together?

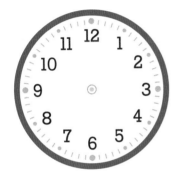 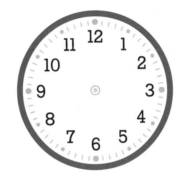

_____ minutes

Alaina placed 52 puzzle pieces, and Zach placed 44 puzzle pieces. How many pieces were in the puzzle in all?

_____ pieces

How many more pieces did Alaina place than Zach?

_____ pieces

The finished puzzle is 24 inches long and 16 inches tall. What is the total length around the edge of the puzzle?

_____ inches

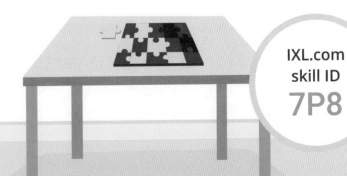

IXL.com
skill ID
7P8

Bradley and Maria work at an indoor game center. Maria records the activities people are doing.

Activity	Number of people
Ball pit	13
Roller skating	32
Rock wall	24
Trampoline	19

Use the table to answer each question.

How many people are using the ball pit or a trampoline?

_____ people

How many people are roller skating or using the rock wall?

_____ people

How many more people are roller skating than using a trampoline?

_____ people

A group of people enter the game center. If 9 of those people go roller skating, how many people are roller skating now?

_____ people

The game center also has a snack bar, and smoothies are the most popular item. Bradley made a pictograph of the smoothie flavors that people ordered.

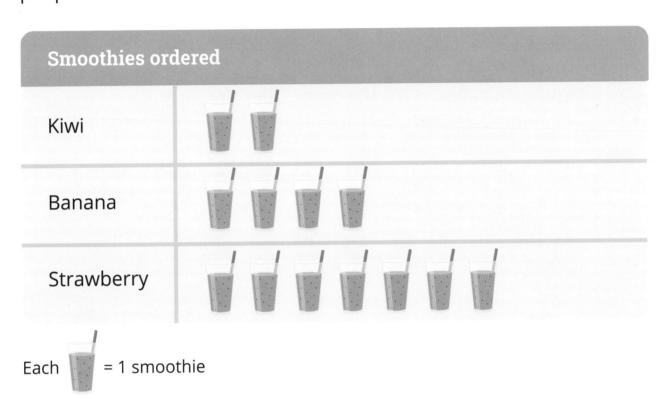

Smoothies ordered

Each 🥤 = 1 smoothie

Answer each question.

Which smoothie flavor was ordered the most? _____

How many banana smoothies did people order? _____ smoothies

How many more strawberry smoothies did people order than kiwi smoothies? _____ smoothies

How many smoothies did people order in all? _____ smoothies

Judy is having a birthday party! Solve each problem.

Judy invited 36 people. If she invited
27 children, how many adults did she invite?   _____ adults

Judy is setting up balloons for the party. There are 5 balloons in each
bunch. Fill in the blanks to skip count by 5.

| 5 | 10 | | 20 | | 30 | | | 45 | |

How many total balloons did Judy set up?   _____ balloons

Judy's mom bought a Happy Birthday
sign to hang on the wall. The sign is
144 inches long. Fill in the blanks with
feet or yards.

The sign is also 12 _____ long or 4 _____ long.

Solve each problem.

Judy's mom filled a piñata with lollipops and chocolate bars. The bags of candy she bought are shown below. Did she buy more lollipops or chocolate bars?

How many candies did Judy's mom buy in all?

_____ candies

The piñata could only hold 205 candies. How many candies were left over?

_____ candies

The bags below show the number of candies some friends got from the piñata. Circle the bags with even numbers.

18   20   13   26   7   14   19

Romeo works at a pizza shop. He made the pizzas shown below. Split each pizza into equal parts.

thirds

fourths

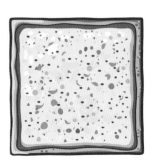

sixths

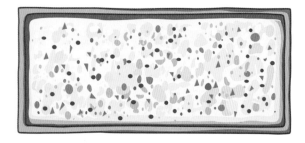

eighths

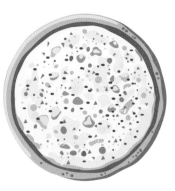

An extra pizza topping costs 85 cents. Is this enough money for an extra topping?

_____

Romeo recorded the number of pizzas he made with each number of toppings.

Pizza toppings	
0 toppings	33 pizzas
1 topping	31 pizzas
2 toppings	22 pizzas
3 toppings	17 pizzas
4 toppings	13 pizzas

Use the table to answer each question.

How many pizzas had 3 or more toppings?   _____ pizzas

How many pizzas had 1 or fewer toppings?   _____ pizzas

How many more pizzas had 2 toppings than 3 toppings?   _____ pizzas

Of all the 1-topping pizzas, 19 had pepperoni. How many did **not** have pepperoni?

_____ pizzas

IXL.com
skill ID

HX2

Answer key

PAGE 2
2 + 5 = 7
5 + 3 = 8
2 + 6 = 8
3 + 7 = 10

PAGE 3
3 + 3 = 6
4 + 5 = 9
6 + 1 = 7

PAGE 4
3 + 6 = 9
4 + 3 = 7
2 + 4 = 6

PAGE 5
1 + 3 = 4
3 + 5 = 8
5 + 4 = 9
2 + 8 = 10
4 + 4 = 8

PAGE 6
6 + 2 = 8   3 + 1 = 4
4 + 4 = 8   5 + 2 = 7
4 + 2 = 6   3 + 2 = 5
1 + 7 = 8   4 + 6 = 10
6 + 3 = 9   3 + 4 = 7
2 + 7 = 9   6 + 1 = 7
4 + 0 = 4   5 + 4 = 9

PAGE 7
7 + 2 = 9   9 + 1 = 10
2 + 3 = 5   0 + 8 = 8
1 + 8 = 9   3 + 5 = 8
8 + 2 = 10   9 + 0 = 9
7 + 1 = 8   2 + 2 = 4
5 + 5 = 10   1 + 5 = 6

PAGE 8
2 + 5 = 7   4 + 2 = 6
5 + 2 = 7   2 + 4 = 6

7 + 2 = 9   8 + 0 = 8
2 + 7 = 9   0 + 8 = 8

9 + 1 = 10   3 + 6 = 9
1 + 9 = 10   6 + 3 = 9

                 7 + 3 = 10
                 3 + 7 = 10

PAGE 9
3 + 4 = 7   4 + 1 = 5
4 + 3 = 7   1 + 4 = 5

5 + 4 = 9   8 + 2 = 10
4 + 5 = 9   2 + 8 = 10

6 + 2 = 8   9 + 0 = 9
2 + 6 = 8   0 + 9 = 9

2 + 3 = 5   1 + 7 = 8
3 + 2 = 5   7 + 1 = 8

PAGE 10
2 + 2 = 4   5 + 5 = 10
3 + 3 = 6   1 + 1 = 2
6 + 6 = 12   4 + 4 = 8
8 + 8 = 16   9 + 9 = 18
7 + 7 = 14   10 + 10 = 20

PAGE 11
3 + 3 = 6   1 + 1 = 2
4 + 4 = 8   6 + 6 = 12
9 + 9 = 18   2 + 2 = 4
5 + 5 = 10   8 + 8 = 16
7 + 7 = 14   10 + 10 = 20

PAGE 12
6 + 6 = 12   4 + 4 = 8   7 + 7 = 14
6 + 7 = 13   4 + 5 = 9   7 + 8 = 15

5 + 5 = 10   9 + 9 = 18   8 + 8 = 16
5 + 6 = 11   9 + 10 = 19 8 + 9 = 17

PAGE 13
5 + 5 = 10   9 + 10 = 19
6 + 7 = 13   4 + 4 = 8
8 + 8 = 16   5 + 6 = 11
7 + 8 = 15   7 + 7 = 14
6 + 6 = 12   9 + 9 = 18
8 + 9 = 17   4 + 5 = 9

PAGE 14
7 + 3 = 10   2 + 8 = 10
6 + 4 = 10   9 + 1 = 10
5 + 5 = 10   8 + 2 = 10
3 + 7 = 10   4 + 6 = 10

10 + 2 = 12   10 + 3 = 13   10 + 6 = 16
10 + 9 = 19   10 + 5 = 15   10 + 10 = 20
10 + 8 = 18   10 + 1 = 11   10 + 7 = 17

PAGE 15

8 + 4 = 10 + 2 = 12

7 + 4 = 10 + 1 = 11

9 + 6 = 10 + 5 = 15

8 + 5 = 10 + 3 = 13

PAGE 16
8 + 6 = 10 + 4 = 14   9 + 2 = 10 + 1 = 11
9 + 4 = 10 + 3 = 13   8 + 7 = 10 + 5 = 15
6 + 5 = 10 + 1 = 11   7 + 6 = 10 + 3 = 13
9 + 3 = 10 + 2 = 12   9 + 8 = 10 + 7 = 17
9 + 9 = 10 + 8 = 18   8 + 3 = 10 + 1 = 11
7 + 5 = 10 + 2 = 12   9 + 7 = 10 + 6 = 16
5 + 9 = 10 + 4 = 14   8 + 4 = 10 + 2 = 12

PAGE 17
9 + 6 = 15   8 + 6 = 14
7 + 4 = 11   5 + 7 = 12
8 + 9 = 17   6 + 9 = 15
9 + 5 = 14   6 + 7 = 13
6 + 8 = 14   8 + 5 = 13
7 + 8 = 15   5 + 6 = 11
5 + 8 = 13   7 + 9 = 16

PAGE 18
3 + 6 = 9   4 + 8 = 12
7 + 7 = 14   3 + 7 = 10
9 + 8 = 17   8 + 6 = 14
5 + 4 = 9   9 + 3 = 12
8 + 7 = 15   3 + 5 = 8
6 + 7 = 13   8 + 2 = 10
8 + 8 = 16   9 + 9 = 18
4 + 7 = 11   9 + 7 = 16

PAGE 19
12 people
14 apples
14 cups
13 pies
17 boards

PAGE 20
6 − 2 = 4
8 − 3 = 5
7 − 4 = 3
10 − 5 = 5

PAGE 21

5 − 4 = 1
8 − 4 = 4
9 − 6 = 3

PAGE 22

7 − 6 = 1
8 − 5 = 3
10 − 3 = 7

PAGE 23

5 − 4 = 1
7 − 5 = 2
9 − 3 = 6
10 − 8 = 2
6 − 3 = 3

PAGE 24

9 − 3 = 6   5 − 2 = 3
8 − 1 = 7   7 − 5 = 2
6 − 5 = 1   4 − 1 = 3
9 − 4 = 5   8 − 2 = 6
10 − 4 = 6   5 − 3 = 2
7 − 2 = 5   10 − 8 = 2
4 − 0 = 4   8 − 6 = 2

PAGE 25

6 − 4 = 2   8 − 5 = 3
3 − 3 = 0   7 − 1 = 6
10 − 6 = 4   10 − 2 = 8
8 − 7 = 1   9 − 6 = 3
6 − 3 = 3   5 − 5 = 0
9 − 7 = 2   9 − 2 = 7
6 − 0 = 6   5 − 1 = 4
9 − 8 = 1   10 − 5 = 5

PAGE 26

9 + 1 = 10   6 + 3 = 9   4 + 4 = 8
10 − 1 = 9   9 − 3 = 6   8 − 4 = 4

5 + 6 = 11   7 + 5 = 12   8 + 7 = 15
11 − 5 = 6   12 − 5 = 7   15 − 8 = 7

PAGE 27

Answers may vary. Some possible answers are shown below.

8 − 5 = 3   6 + 1 = 7
9 − 3 = 6   13 − 9 = 4
8 + 5 = 13   11 − 6 = 5
9 + 7 = 16   6 + 9 = 15
9 + 9 = 18   15 − 7 = 8

PAGE 28

Order of facts may vary.

2 + 9 = 11   3 + 4 = 7
9 + 2 = 11   4 + 3 = 7
11 − 2 = 9   7 − 4 = 3
11 − 9 = 2   7 − 3 = 4

PAGE 29

Order of facts may vary.

4 + 8 = 12   5 + 7 = 12
8 + 4 = 12   7 + 5 = 12
12 − 4 = 8   12 − 5 = 7
12 − 8 = 4   12 − 7 = 5

7 + 8 = 15   9 + 8 = 17
8 + 7 = 15   8 + 9 = 17
15 − 7 = 8   17 − 9 = 8
15 − 8 = 7   17 − 8 = 9

9 + 10 = 19   6 + 8 = 14
10 + 9 = 19   8 + 6 = 14
19 − 10 = 9   14 − 6 = 8
19 − 9 = 10   14 − 8 = 6

PAGE 30

10 − 4 = 6   10 − 2 = 8
10 − 1 = 9   10 − 7 = 3
10 − 5 = 5   10 − 8 = 2
17 − 7 = 10   11 − 1 = 10
18 − 8 = 10   19 − 9 = 10
16 − 6 = 10   13 − 3 = 10
10 − 0 = 10   14 − 4 = 10

PAGE 31

15 − 8 = ?
15 − 5 − 3 = ?
10 − 3 = 7

16 − 8 = ?
16 − 6 − 2 = ?
10 − 2 = 8

14 − 9 = ?
14 − 4 − 5 = ?
10 − 5 = 5

PAGE 32

13 − 6 = ?
13 − 3 − 3 = ?
10 − 3 = 7

15 − 6 = ?
15 − 5 − 1 = ?
10 − 1 = 9

PAGE 32, continued

13 − 4 = ?   14 − 5 = ?
13 − 3 − 1 = ?   14 − 4 − 1 = ?
10 − 1 = 9   10 − 1 = 9

15 − 7 = ?   16 − 9 = ?
15 − 5 − 2 = ?   16 − 6 − 3 = ?
10 − 2 = 8   10 − 3 = 7

14 − 6 = ?   17 − 8 = ?
14 − 4 − 2 = ?   17 − 7 − 1 = ?
10 − 2 = 8   10 − 1 = 9

PAGE 33

13 − 5 = 8   14 − 5 = 9
13 − 7 = 6   15 − 6 = 9
14 − 9 = 5   12 − 5 = 7
14 − 6 = 8   17 − 8 = 9
12 − 4 = 8   15 − 9 = 6
16 − 9 = 7   12 − 8 = 4
17 − 9 = 8   16 − 7 = 9
15 − 7 = 8   14 − 8 = 6

PAGE 34

16 − 5 = 11   7 + 7 = 14
6 + 4 = 10   11 − 6 = 5
8 + 7 = 15   5 + 9 = 14
17 − 8 = 9   12 − 6 = 6
13 − 5 = 8   7 + 4 = 11
4 + 8 = 12   15 − 7 = 8
14 − 6 = 8   9 + 9 = 18

PAGE 35

5 + 8 = 13   9 + 3 = 12
12 − 7 = 5   13 − 4 = 9
16 − 9 = 7   2 + 8 = 10
3 + 7 = 10   15 − 6 = 9
17 − 7 = 10   12 − 8 = 4
13 − 2 = 11   8 + 6 = 14
11 − 8 = 3   8 + 8 = 16

PAGE 36

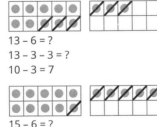

Answer key

PAGE 37

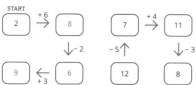

PAGE 38
6 coins
9 coins
No, she has 3 coins left.

PAGE 39
8 tickets
14 tickets
8 tickets

PAGE 40
17 + 5 = 22
15 + 6 = 21
19 + 6 = 25
16 + 7 = 23

PAGE 41
18 + 4 = 22   20 + 4 = 24
14 + 6 = 20   19 + 2 = 21
17 + 7 = 24   16 + 5 = 21
18 + 5 = 23   19 + 4 = 23
16 + 4 = 20   13 + 9 = 22
19 + 6 = 25   22 + 3 = 25
17 + 6 = 23   18 + 6 = 24

PAGE 42
(6 + 4) + 7 = 10 + 7 = 17
6 + (4 + 7) = 6 + 11 = 17

(1 + 9) + 8 = 10 + 8 = 18
1 + (9 + 8) = 1 + 17 = 18

(6 + 6) + 5 = 12 + 5 = 17
6 + (6 + 5) = 6 + 11 = 17

(8 + 7) + 9 = 15 + 9 = 24
8 + (7 + 9) = 8 + 16 = 24

(9 + 9) + 5 = 18 + 5 = 23
9 + (9 + 5) = 9 + 14 = 23

(5 + 8) + 8 = 13 + 8 = 21
5 + (8 + 8) = 5 + 16 = 21

The easier rows are those with adjacent numbers that form a double, a near double, or a 10.

PAGE 43
3 + 7 + 7 = 17   3 + 5 + 4 = 12
8 + 4 + 3 = 15   6 + 4 + 2 = 12
7 + 3 + 2 = 12   6 + 6 + 4 = 16
9 + 3 + 7 = 19   5 + 7 + 4 = 16
4 + 8 + 8 = 20   2 + 8 + 9 = 19
9 + 4 + 9 = 22   6 + 8 + 7 = 21
3 + 8 + 7 = 18   8 + 9 + 5 = 22

PAGE 44
4 + 4 + 8 + 2 = 18   6 + 2 + 7 + 3 = 18
3 + 8 + 7 + 7 = 25   1 + 9 + 7 + 5 = 22
6 + 2 + 8 + 5 = 21   9 + 6 + 5 + 5 = 25
7 + 2 + 9 + 3 = 21   9 + 3 + 1 + 2 = 15
8 + 3 + 5 + 6 = 22   6 + 6 + 5 + 2 = 19
3 + 6 + 4 + 3 = 16   4 + 6 + 8 + 7 = 25

PAGE 45

7	9	2
3	4	1
8	6	5

1	9	7
3	4	6
5	8	2

9	8	2
7	4	3
6	5	1

9	4	2
8	6	3
1	7	5

PAGE 46
17 flowers
19 people
16 fish

PAGE 47
2 + 2 + 2 = 6   5 + 5 + 5 = 15
6 + 6 + 6 = 18   3 + 3 + 3 = 9
8 + 8 + 8 = 24   7 + 7 + 7 = 21
10 + 10 + 10 = 30   9 + 9 + 9 = 27

PAGE 48
6 + 6 + 6 = 18
5 + 5 + 5 + 5 = 20
6 + 6 + 6 + 6 = 24

PAGE 49
8 + 8 + 8 = 24
3 + 3 + 3 + 3 = 12
4 + 4 + 4 + 4 = 16
7 + 7 + 7 = 21

PAGE 50
18 ears of corn   20 heads of broccoli
10 tomatoes   24 pumpkins

PAGE 51
20 cows
18 horses
15 goats
21 pieces of wood
16 tires

PAGE 52
3 × 2 = 6 mittens

PAGE 53
5 × 2 = 10 toothbrushes
3 × 4 = 12 muffins
2 × 4 = 8 cars

PAGE 54
22 + 5 = 27   34 + 4 = 38
42 + 7 = 49   55 + 3 = 58

PAGE 55
23 + 4 = 27   36 + 3 = 39
41 + 8 = 49   44 + 5 = 49
64 + 3 = 67   51 + 7 = 58

PAGE 56
37 + 2 = 39   23 + 6 = 29
24 + 5 = 29   31 + 7 = 38
42 + 3 = 45   28 + 1 = 29
56 + 2 = 58   41 + 5 = 46
64 + 4 = 68   53 + 4 = 57
72 + 6 = 78   86 + 3 = 89

PAGE 57
32 + 25 = 57   21 + 15 = 36
24 + 14 = 38   33 + 13 = 46
23 + 16 = 39   47 + 12 = 59

PAGE 58
32 + 23 = 55   41 + 24 = 65
35 + 42 = 77   53 + 26 = 79
42 + 31 = 73   62 + 22 = 84

PAGE 59
12 + 14 = 26   34 + 13 = 47
23 + 25 = 48   17 + 22 = 39
36 + 23 = 59   43 + 24 = 67
32 + 21 = 53   31 + 48 = 79
33 + 52 = 85   42 + 46 = 88
54 + 35 = 89   56 + 22 = 78
67 + 11 = 78   54 + 45 = 99

PAGE 60
36 + 7 = 40 + 3 = 43   24 + 7 = 30 + 1 = 31
39 + 5 = 40 + 4 = 44   28 + 8 = 30 + 6 = 36

PAGE 61

56 + 9 = 60 + 5 = 65   26 + 5 = 30 + 1 = 31
38 + 4 = 40 + 2 = 42   47 + 7 = 50 + 4 = 54
76 + 8 = 80 + 4 = 84   33 + 9 = 40 + 2 = 42
65 + 6 = 70 + 1 = 71   54 + 8 = 60 + 2 = 62

49 + 4 = 53   78 + 5 = 83
32 + 9 = 41   26 + 6 = 32
67 + 5 = 72   53 + 8 = 61
88 + 3 = 91   75 + 9 = 84

PAGE 62

45   22   72
+ 23   + 65   + 21
68   87   93

31   24   33
+ 48   + 24   + 44
79   48   77

PAGE 63

23   37   32
+ 35   + 12   + 34
58   49   66

42   51   42
+ 22   + 38   + 42
64   89   84

73   12   43
+ 24   + 71   + 36
97   83   79

84   15   24
+ 14   + 41   + 63
98   56   87

33   64   62
+ 32   + 35   + 16
65   99   78

32   55
+ 62   + 43
94   98

PAGE 64

46   28   19
+ 35   + 14   + 36
81   42   55

33   59   48
+ 57   + 39   + 36
90   98   84

PAGE 65

26   24   65
+ 17   + 38   + 27
43   62   92

39   77   38
+ 41   + 16   + 29
80   93   67

79   32   56
+ 12   + 19   + 26
91   51   82

68   27   79
+ 27   + 47   + 15
95   74   94

PAGE 66

27   42   38
+ 45   + 36   + 33
72   78   71

52   26   39
+ 47   + 64   + 14
99   90   53

53   48   35
+ 24   + 48   + 36
77   96   71

64   26   54
+ 27   + 39   + 22
91   65   76

36   18   71
+ 43   + 64   + 25
79   82   96

PAGE 67

49   28   (26
+ 16   + 36   + 52
65   64   78)

54   (48   39
+ 24   + 33   + 19
78   81)   58

29   (23   36
+ 44   + 52   + 35
73   75)   71

(37   14   28
+ 54   + 76   + 58
91)   90   86

16   27   (18
+ 63   + 49   + 62
79   76   80)

PAGE 68

```
      64                     90
   28    36               41    49
 13   15   21           24   17   32

      74                     99
   23    51               48    51
 14    9   42           29   19   32

      95                     98
   55    40               58    40
 47    8   32           36   22   18
```

PAGE 69

START↓ FINISH↓

55 + 28 = 83	68 + 26 = 94	21 + 40 = 61	39 + 48 = 87	57 + 17 = 74
44 + 15 = 59	14 + 28 = 42	24 + 17 = 41	57 + 25 = 82	29 + 29 = 58
36 + 16 = 52	44 + 55 = 99	63 + 21 = 84	45 + 38 = 83	46 + 22 = 68
59 + 39 = 98	46 + 43 = 89	65 + 27 = 92	57 + 22 = 79	62 + 19 = 81
74 + 19 = 93	29 + 35 = 64	59 + 20 = 79	81 + 13 = 94	44 + 28 = 72

PAGE 70

61 blocks
48 children
76 minutes
72 pieces

PAGE 71

$77
86 feet
52 riders

PAGE 72

27 – 4 = 23   36 – 6 = 30
49 – 8 = 41   68 – 5 = 63

PAGE 73

24 – 2 = 22   38 – 3 = 35
47 – 5 = 42   54 – 4 = 50
75 – 4 = 71   69 – 7 = 62

PAGE 74

25 – 4 = 21   36 – 3 = 33
44 – 2 = 42   38 – 1 = 37
59 – 5 = 54   47 – 6 = 41
67 – 7 = 60   54 – 3 = 51
89 – 8 = 81   72 – 2 = 70

PAGE 75

28 – 11 = 17   37 – 22 = 15
46 – 16 = 30   55 – 34 = 21

PAGE 76

34 – 11 = 23   56 – 35 = 21
48 – 24 = 24   53 – 12 = 41
65 – 15 = 50   47 – 34 = 13

Answer key

PAGE 77

34 − 21 = 13   39 − 15 = 24
63 − 22 = 41   79 − 43 = 36
58 − 41 = 17   37 − 25 = 12
49 − 27 = 22   56 − 34 = 22
67 − 32 = 35   73 − 31 = 42

PAGE 79

33 − 5 = 28   24 − 8 = 16
73 − 4 = 69   42 − 7 = 35
66 − 9 = 57   71 − 6 = 65

PAGE 80

| 45 − 23 = 22 | 54 − 13 = 41 | 63 − 31 = 32 |
| 68 − 21 = 47 | 75 − 32 = 43 | 48 − 17 = 31 |

PAGE 81

48 − 23 = 25	56 − 12 = 44	33 − 22 = 11
65 − 34 = 31	47 − 24 = 23	59 − 27 = 32
78 − 41 = 37	69 − 54 = 15	46 − 33 = 13
84 − 13 = 71	52 − 21 = 31	85 − 52 = 33
97 − 56 = 41	67 − 41 = 26	68 − 45 = 23
96 − 42 = 54	39 − 23 = 16	

PAGE 82

| 55 − 18 = 37 | 38 − 19 = 19 | 45 − 28 = 17 |
| 62 − 35 = 27 | 73 − 27 = 46 | 84 − 39 = 45 |

PAGE 83

63 − 26 = 37	86 − 57 = 29	75 − 67 = 8
42 − 24 = 18	74 − 38 = 36	56 − 28 = 28
82 − 45 = 37	92 − 67 = 25	80 − 47 = 33
41 − 18 = 23	87 − 49 = 38	50 − 36 = 14

PAGE 84

29 − 18 = 11	35 − 22 = 13	(42 − 34 = 8)
(74 − 58 = 16)	56 − 25 = 31	67 − 39 = 28
(49 − 29 = 20)	70 − 42 = 28	84 − 55 = 29
98 − 69 = 29	(64 − 38 = 26)	56 − 27 = 29
76 − 27 = 49	85 − 32 = 53	(57 − 19 = 38)

PAGE 85

76 − 31 = 45	84 − 63 = 21	76 − 32 = 44
86 − 49 = 37	89 − 54 = 35	82 − 43 = 39
97 − 68 = 29	40 − 17 = 23	66 − 18 = 48

PAGE 86

13 minutes
22 shots
$44
57 baked goods

PAGE 87

33 campers
26 campers
19 feet

PAGE 88

65 + 23 = 88	48 − 23 = 25	78 − 36 = 42
36 + 41 = 77	83 − 27 = 56	33 + 34 = 67
42 − 25 = 17	67 − 18 = 49	57 + 23 = 80
91 − 38 = 53	25 + 57 = 82	53 + 38 = 91

PAGE 89

34 + 39 = 73	61 + 12 = 73	92 − 19 = 73	97 − 38 = 59	43 + 16 = 59	32 + 25 = 57
95 − 22 = 73	64 + 12 = 76	83 − 16 = 67	27 + 31 = 58	83 − 24 = 59	29 + 28 = 57
83 − 20 = 63	32 + 51 = 83	79 − 26 = 53	72 − 23 = 49	17 + 42 = 59	70 − 21 = 49
29 − 25 = 4	91 − 25 = 66	39 + 27 = 66	39 + 29 = 68	82 − 14 = 68	55 + 12 = 67
92 − 25 = 67	94 − 12 = 82	19 + 48 = 67	90 − 23 = 67	27 + 42 = 69	95 − 28 = 67
87 − 29 = 58	75 − 17 = 58	49 − 33 = 82	27 + 41 = 68	87 − 19 = 68	49 + 19 = 68

PAGE 90

42 flavors
14 candies
31 jumps
18 blocks

PAGE 91

Rule: add 26	
In	Out
22	48
35	61
57	83

Rule: subtract 23	
In	Out
35	12
54	31
62	39

Rule: add 54	
In	Out
14	68
27	81
36	90

Rule: subtract 37	
In	Out
43	6
51	14
79	42

PAGE 92

Rule: add 21	
In	Out
19	40
30	51
57	78

Rule: subtract 29	
In	Out
35	6
59	30
77	48

Rule: subtract 25	
In	Out
32	7
49	24
66	41

Rule: add 28	
In	Out
17	45
26	54
38	66

Rule: subtract 59	
In	Out
61	2
72	13
84	25

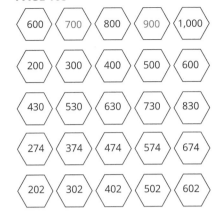

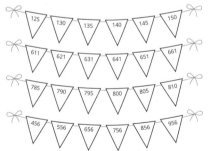

PAGE 93

add 34

subtract 37

add 74

subtract 14

add 26

PAGE 94

even

odd

odd

even

7   ②

13   ⑥

1   ⑩

3   15

PAGE 95

4③ odd

7⓪ even

2⑦ odd

1 2⑨ odd

6 5⑧ even

5⑥ even

6④ even

9① odd

2 1② even

9 4⑤ odd

PAGE 96

odd + even = odd   even + even = even

odd + odd = even   even + odd = odd

even + even = even   odd + odd = even

even

even

odd

PAGE 97

odd   even

odd   odd

even   odd

even   even

odd

even

even

PAGE 98

347

424

192

PAGE 99

371

406

216

340

153

PAGE 100

tens   50

hundreds   900

ones   3

hundreds   200

tens   30

ones   7

tens   10

PAGE 101

207 = 200 + 7

820 = 800 + 20

438 = 400 + 30 + 8

446 = 400 + 40 + 6

671 = 600 + 70 + 1

563 = 500 + 60 + 3

926 = 900 + 20 + 6

103 = 100 + 3

317 = 300 + 10 + 7

560 = 500 + 60

PAGE 102

300 + 60 + 7 = 367

800 + 20 + 3 = 823

700 + 60 + 2 = 762

400 + 5 = 405

900 + 10 + 6 = 916

500 + 20 = 520

400 + 90 + 1 = 491

600 + 10 + 4 = 614

200 + 90 + 5 = 295

800 + 70 = 870

700 + 60 + 8 = 768

300 + 9 = 309

PAGE 103

356

760

939

491

one hundred seventy-three

eight hundred twenty-one

nine hundred four

five hundred fourteen

one hundred eighty

PAGE 104

10	20	30	40	50
70	80	90	100	110
340	350	360	370	380
22	32	42	52	62
736	746	756	766	776

The digit in the ones place stays the same. The digit in the tens place goes up by 1.

PAGE 105

600	700	800	900	1,000
200	300	400	500	600
430	530	630	730	830
274	374	474	574	674
202	302	402	502	602

The digit in the ones place stays the same. The digit in the tens place stays the same. The digit in the hundreds place goes up by 1.

PAGE 106

5	10	15	20	25
45	50	55	60	65
120	125	130	135	140
255	260	265	270	275
480	485	490	495	500
690	695	700	705	710

The ones digit alternates between 0 and 5.

PAGE 107

125 130 135 140 145 150

611 621 631 641 651 661

785 790 795 800 805 810

456 556 656 756 856 956

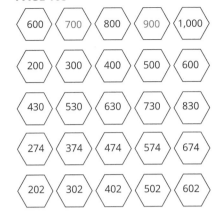

217

Answer key

PAGE 108

382 is greater than 294.
382 > 294

467 is less than 521.
467 < 521

872 is greater than 728.
872 > 728

302 is equal to 302.
302 = 302

PAGE 109

419 > 194   824 > 428
783 < 837   365 < 563
507 = 507   915 < 951
812 < 879   322 > 313

Answers may vary. Some possible answers are shown below.

345 < 479   337 > 329
401 < 501   583 < 592
685 = 685

PAGE 110

247 + 251 = 498	234 + 362 = 596	625 + 204 = 829
485 + 102 = 587	216 + 423 = 639	321 + 320 = 641
746 + 240 = 986	227 + 552 = 779	833 + 164 = 997

PAGE 111

427 + 213 = 640	251 + 173 = 424	509 + 116 = 625
324 + 287 = 611	449 + 248 = 697	255 + 276 = 531
534 + 187 = 721	486 + 486 = 972	

PAGE 112

170 + 427 = 597	251 + 119 = 370	355 + 203 = 558
241 + 188 = 429	375 + 125 = 500	263 + 645 = 908
448 + 312 = 760	593 + 126 = 719	285 + 377 = 662
634 + 223 = 857	149 + 756 = 905	474 + 308 = 782

PAGE 113

126 + 235 = 361	247 + 201 = 448	368 + 124 = 492
556 + 341 = 897	605 + 199 = 804	243 + 547 = 790
339 + 339 = 678	478 + 205 = 683	216 + 284 = 500
439 + 269 = 708	467 + 278 = 745	755 + 195 = 950
587 + 296 = 883	776 + 187 = 963	586 + 259 = 845

PAGE 114

```
        286
     107    161
   49    58    103
```
```
        442
     251    191
   142   109   82
```
```
        791
     407    384
   212   195   189
```
```
        839
     488    351
   392   96    255
```
```
        938
     571    367
   413   158   209
```
```
        984
     501    483
   137   364   119
```

PAGE 115

213 pictures
815 pounds
410 cupcakes
$914

PAGE 116

562 − 151 = 411	456 − 213 = 243	326 − 121 = 205
674 − 523 = 151	947 − 425 = 522	898 − 704 = 194
709 − 603 = 106	996 − 384 = 612	693 − 472 = 221

PAGE 117

439 − 229 = 210	716 − 302 = 414	583 − 261 = 322
984 − 582 = 402	874 − 250 = 624	338 − 215 = 123
649 − 627 = 22	288 − 153 = 135	499 − 387 = 112
982 − 261 = 721	564 − 162 = 402	887 − 456 = 431

PAGE 119

754 − 159 = 595	592 − 273 = 319	693 − 286 = 407
825 − 378 = 447	362 − 123 = 239	778 − 189 = 589
714 − 624 = 90	831 − 469 = 362	513 − 279 = 234
605 − 379 = 226	803 − 546 = 257	602 − 254 = 348
906 − 138 = 768	400 − 114 = 286	

PAGE 120

895 − 106 = 789	653 − 277 = 376	924 − 659 = 265
568 − 298 = 270	925 − 549 = 376	761 − 508 = 253
713 − 407 = 306	922 − 608 = 314	500 − 238 = 262
527 − 346 = 181	781 − 225 = 556	646 − 385 = 261
800 − 543 = 257	479 − 189 = 290	514 − 298 = 216

PAGE 121

102 > 68
485 > 315
358 < 362
389 > 386

PAGE 122

345 seats
$111
151 miles
76 pieces

PAGE 123

405 + 391 796	564 – 323 241	348 – 256 92
683 + 229 912	478 + 513 991	573 – 264 309
744 – 356 388	253 – 179 74	465 + 275 740
608 + 297 905	621 – 345 276	346 + 247 593
379 + 338 717	904 – 586 318	750 – 476 274
686 + 135 821	592 + 348 940	911 – 598 313

PAGE 124

784 – 297 487	346 + 355 701	631 – 428 203
290 + 148 438	573 + 387 960	402 – 151 251
632 + 274 906	511 – 343 168	329 + 489 818
903 – 526 377	434 – 378 56	175 + 335 510
318 – 276 42	269 + 463 732	548 – 268 280

PAGE 125

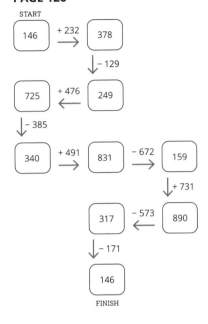

PAGE 126

START

146 → + 232 → 378

↓ – 129

725 ← + 476 ← 249

↓ – 385

340 → + 491 → 831 → – 672 → 159

↓ + 731

317 ← – 573 ← 890

↓ – 171

146

FINISH

PAGE 127

215 people
240 pretzels
423 campers
73 stones

PAGE 128

4 inches
3 inches 2 inches
5 inches

PAGE 129

3 centimeters 5 centimeters
14 centimeters
10 centimeters

PAGE 130

about 3 inches about 2 inches
about 5 inches

PAGE 131

about 3 centimeters
about 8 centimeters
about 6 centimeters
about 14 centimeters

PAGE 132

A doorway is about 8 feet tall.
A bookmark is about 8 inches long.
A car is about 5 yards long.
A bed is about 7 feet long.
A cup is about 4 inches tall.

PAGE 133

6 feet 4 inches
8 feet 15 yards
3 inches 8 inches
7 inches 2 yards

PAGE 134

A pen is about 12 centimeters long.
A couch is about 3 meters long.
A water bottle is about 20 centimeters tall.
The stick on a mop is about 2 meters long.
A minivan is about 5 meters long.
A soup can is about 10 centimeters tall.

PAGE 135

8 centimeters 20 meters
7 centimeters 16 centimeters
10 centimeters 30 centimeters
14 meters 12 meters

PAGE 136

5 inches
4 inches
6 inches
3 inches

PAGE 137

7 centimeters 8 centimeters
4 centimeters 2 centimeters
13 centimeters

PAGE 139

Height of a chair	
about 48 inches	about 4 feet

Length of a horse	
about 3 yards	about 9 feet

Height of a stop sign	
about 5 feet	about 60 inches

Length of a fire truck	
about 36 feet	about 12 yards

Height of a goose	
about 1 yard	about 3 feet

PAGE 140

Length of a park bench	
about 2 meters	about 200 centimeters

Height of a flagpole	
about 5 meters	about 500 centimeters

Length of golf club	
about 100 centimeters	about 1 meter

Height of an elephant	
about 400 centimeters	about 4 meters

PAGE 141
74 feet   66 inches
52 meters   44 yards

PAGE 142
52 inches   24 yards
35 feet   62 meters

PAGE 143
41 inches
58 yards
80 meters
28 minutes

PAGE 144
6 centimeters
36 meters
95 centimeters
102 yards

PAGE 145
Tony is 56 inches tall.
Gia is 53 inches tall.
Stephanie is 62 inches tall.
Eli is 42 inches tall.
Sean is 48 inches tall.

PAGE 146
10¢	20¢	21¢	Total value: 21¢
10¢	15¢	20¢	Total value: 20¢
25¢	50¢	55¢	Total value: 55¢

PAGE 147
25¢	35¢	45¢	50¢	Total value: 50¢
25¢	35¢	40¢	41¢	Total value: 41¢
10¢	20¢	25¢	26¢	Total value: 26¢
25¢	30¢	31¢	32¢	Total value: 32¢
10¢	20¢	25¢	30¢	Total value: 30¢

PAGE 148
36¢   37¢
56¢   80¢
It is usually easier to start with quarters and count on from there.

PAGE 149
71¢   42¢
47¢   91¢

PAGE 150
1 dime, 1 nickel
3 dimes
2 nickels, 1 penny
2 quarters, 1 dime
4¢

PAGE 151
$20	$30	$35	Total value: $35
$20	$25	$26	Total value: $26

PAGE 152
$20	$30	$35	$40	Total value: $40
$20	$40	$45	$50	Total value: $50
$10	$15	$16	$17	Total value: $17
$20	$40	$50	$55	Total value: $55

PAGE 153
$31 $21
$70 $27
$26 $51

PAGE 154
$72 $67
$76 $75

PAGE 155
$42, Max
$34, Jerry
$57, Sandy

PAGE 156
$5.07
$10.25
$2.11
$20.03

PAGE 157

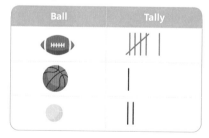

PAGE 157, continued

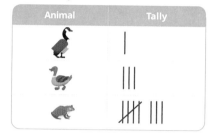

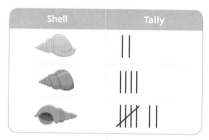

PAGE 158

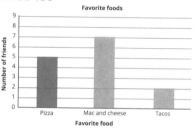

PAGE 159

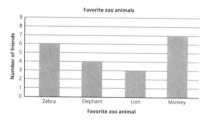

PAGE 160
4 people
a park
the beach
4 people

PAGE 161
7 cakes
lemon
3 cakes
23 cakes

PAGE 162

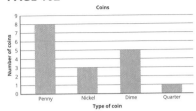

PAGE 163

15¢
50¢
nickels
dimes
10¢
42¢
98¢

PAGE 164

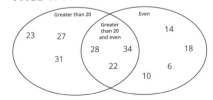

PAGE 165

(See below for clocks)

PAGE 166

plastic
2 glass items
3 paper items
13 items

PAGE 167

6 people
fall and spring
winter
11 people

PAGE 168

2 friends
3 friends
6 friends
10 friends

PAGE 169

2 pets
4 friends
4 friends
3 friends

PAGE 170

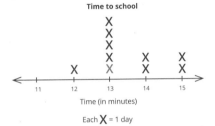

PAGE 171

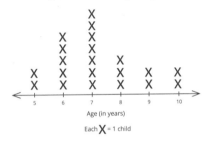

PAGE 172

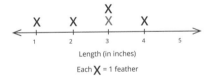

PAGE 173

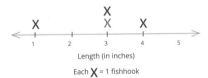

PAGE 174

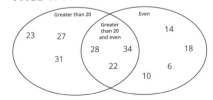

PAGE 175

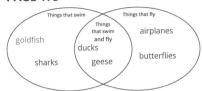

PAGE 176

1:30	8:00
4:00	10:30
7:30	12:00

PAGE 177

7:45	10:10	4:15
5:05	8:35	

PAGE 178

Answer key

PAGE 179

PAGE 180

quarter past 3
10 minutes after 2
half past 11

half past 6
5 minutes to 4
quarter to 1

PAGE 181

4:50
Carmen is early for painting class.
6:20
6:30
quarter to 7

PAGE 182

p.m.   a.m.
a.m.   p.m.
p.m.   a.m.

PAGE 183

a.m.

The weather will be sunny.
1:30
half past 1

PAGE 184

PAGE 185

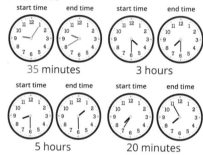

PAGE 186

3	4	4
6	3	6
7	10	6

PAGE 187

hexagon   quadrilateral   triangle
pentagon   hexagon   quadrilateral

PAGE 188

pentagon
triangle
quadrilateral

hexagon
pentagon
triangle

quadrilateral
hexagon
pentagon

PAGE 189

Drawings may vary. Some possible answers are shown below.

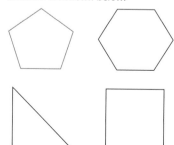

PAGE 189, continued

Drawings may vary. Some possible answers are shown below.

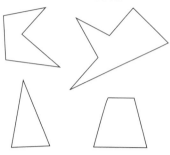

PAGE 190

5	4
3	6
5	5

PAGE 191

Drawings may vary. Some possible answers are shown below.

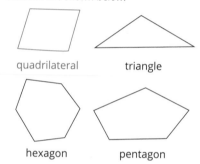

quadrilateral   triangle

hexagon   pentagon

The number of sides in a shape is the same as the number of angles. A shape with 10 angles would have 10 sides.

PAGE 192

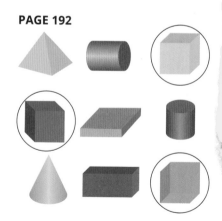

PAGE 193

PAGE 194

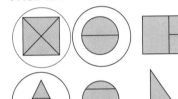

PAGE 195

fourths	halves	thirds
thirds	fourths	

PAGE 196

Drawings may vary. Some possible answers are shown below.

PAGE 197

one half	one fourth	one third
one fourth	one third	one half

PAGE 198

Drawings may vary. Some possible answers are shown below.

PAGE 199

Drawings may vary. Some possible answers are shown below.

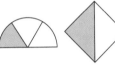

PAGE 200

sixths	sixths	eighths
one eighth	one sixth	one eighth

PAGE 201

Shading may vary. Some possible answers are shown below.

PAGE 202

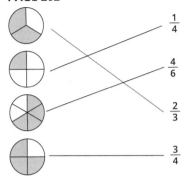

$\frac{1}{4}$

$\frac{4}{6}$

$\frac{2}{3}$

$\frac{3}{4}$

PAGE 203

$\frac{1}{3}$	$\frac{2}{4}$
$\frac{2}{6}$	$\frac{1}{2}$
$\frac{3}{4}$	$\frac{5}{8}$

PAGE 204

$8
80¢

PAGE 205

25 minutes
96 pieces
8 pieces
80 inches

PAGE 206

32 people
56 people
13 people
41 people

PAGE 207

strawberry
4 smoothies
5 smoothies
13 smoothies

PAGE 208

9 adults

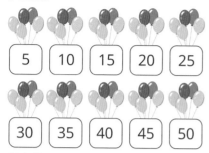

5 10 15 20 25

30 35 40 45 50

50 balloons
The sign is also 12 feet long or 4 yards long.

PAGE 209

lollipops
277 candies
72 candies

18 20 13 26 7 14 19

PAGE 210

Answers may vary. Some possible answers are shown below.

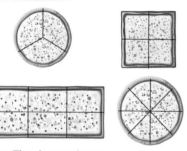

Yes. The change shown is 85 cents.

PAGE 211

30 pizzas
64 pizzas
5 pizzas
12 pizzas